DO YOU BELIEVE THAT JESUS CAN HEAL YOU?

by

Margaret M. Trosclair, S.O.S.M.

Mary's Helpers Publishing Company
P.O. Box 1853
Marrero, LA 70072
(504) 348-PRAY (7729)
Fax (504) 347-7715

Published by Mary's Helpers, Inc.
For additional copies, write:

Mary's Helpers, Inc.
PO Box 1853
Marrero, LA 70072

ISBN: 0-9649001-1-4

INTRODUCTION

In June, 1981, Mary, the Mother of God, began to appear to six children in Yugoslavia. When I first became aware of this village, I tried to get there. Because of the uprising in Yugoslavia, I was not able to make my first pilgrimage until 1986. I was thrilled to be present during the Feasts of the Triumph of the Cross and Our Lady of Sorrows.

My first meeting with Father Peter Mary Rookey, O.S.M. took place in the cemetery in Medjugorje. Our group of about one hundred would meet there each day following the English Mass for a talk given by someone from St. James Church on the current events surrounding the six children since the apparitions began. One day at the church, my friend, Frances LaFont, witnessed the healing of a twelve year old boy through Father Rookey. Shortly after, Frances brought Father Rookey and the boy to give witness to our group in the cemetery.

After returning from Medjugorje in September 1986, I started giving talks. In February, 1987 I organized Mary's Helpers. Inc., which is a non-profit organization dedicated to spreading the messages of Jesus and His mother, Mary. We do this through a monthly newsletter, and our weekly radio talk show with six programs on four stations.

When it came time for the sixth Anniversary of the apparitions, I returned to Medjugorje. During this pilgrimage, Our Blessed Mother, the Mother of Jesus, gave me the grace to do the enhancement of Her statue in St. James Church which is the parish church. I was a costume and apparel designer for many years, and I longed to give back to God some of the gifts He had given to me. After the anniversary, I felt called to bring a replica of the statue of Our Lady of Lourdes home for those people who would never have a chance to visit Medjugorje to see the original. After six months of intense prayer, Father Richard Maughan, Pastor of The Visitation of Our Lady Church in Marrero, Louisiana, consented to enthrone the statue that I had carved in Ortisei, Italy.

I had not seen or heard from or about Father Rookey again until Cathy McCarthy, who was on my first pilgrimage, phoned from Las Vegas. She called to tell me Father Rookey had given a wonderful healing service in her home town. After telling her about the plans for the celebration of the enthronement, she suggested that I should invite Father Rookey to be my guest. Father Maughan was against inviting Father Rookey, and suggested a list of more suitable candidates for such a special occasion as this one. Shortly after, Father Maughan was preparing for a trip to Ireland because his mother had been involved in an automobile accident. I went to Father to report to him that no one had responded affirmatively to our invitation. I again asked him about Father Rookey, and he agreed. When I contacted Father Rookey, he already knew that he was coming to the enthronement celebration. I was astounded because I had not invited him.

The three day celebration began Thursday, October 6, 1988 with the unveiling of the statue of Our Lady of Lourdes of Medjugorje at The Visitation of Our Lady Church. On Friday, October 7, 1988, a candlelight procession had approximately three thousand people walking from St. John Bosco Church in Harvey to Visitation in Marrero carrying the statue of Our Lady on a bier. Approximately seventeen hundred people lined the streets for the procession while another three hundred waited for us at Visitation Church.

Since that time, all of us at Mary's Helpers have worked closely with Father Rookey. We have fallen in love with the charism of the Servite Order, and the devotions to Our Lady of Sorrows. In February, 1989, my husband, Harold, and I went to Chicago to meet with Father Rookey and others from different parts of the country to begin communities of the Secular Order of the Servants of Mary. After seven years and a great deal of prayers, our prayers were finally answered. We began the Secular Servite community in January, 1995. September 7, 1991 was the beginning of our annual Solemn Novena of Our Lady of Sorrows at Immaculate Conception Church in Marrero, Louisiana. Each year we end the novena with a Rosary Procession on September 15, the Feast of Our Lady of Sorrows.

On November 9, 1992, Mary's Helpers was accepted into the Secular Order. The official letter of acceptance arrived at Mary's Helpers on November 16, 1992, the feast day of Saint Margaret of Scotland and Saint Gertrude, Gayle Ponseti's and my feast day, but we were unable to secure a spiritual director. At the close of the 1994 Novena, Father Alberto Bermudez offered to do something special for Mary's Helpers. Because he was so impressed with the conversions the novena brought about, as well as the number of people who attended, he knew he had to become involved. After four solemn novenas, Jesus granted our petition by sending Father Alberto to us as our spiritual director. We are the first Secular Order of the Servants of Mary to begin in the South and, for us, it is a historical event. Our thanks go to Father Peter Mary Rookey, O.S.M. for being our inspiration, and for introducing us to Our Mother of Sorrows.

When I began to write this story, I mentioned that I met Father Rookey in September when I was in Medjugorje for the Feast of Our Lady of Sorrows. Ever since that day, I can see how the pieces of the puzzle are fitting together.

It is a great privilege to be able to write this book about a man who has given his life to God unquestionably. He brings Jesus to everyone he meets through healing and hope. This book was begun about three years ago, and I know now that it is time for it to be published. The Lord sent me all the people I needed to complete it. The thoughts, ideas and words contained within are all Father Rookey's.

Margaret M. Trosclair, S.O.S.M.

Acknowledgments

Without Father Rookey' s blessing this book would not have been possible. He has helped us spread the message of Jesus and Mary through God's gift to him in his healing ministry. Father will always be remembered in our prayers.

Many thanks to Elson Legendre for accepting without blinking an eye when I mentioned I needed help to put the wealth of data I had on Father Rookey into the computer.

Morgan Legendre, Elson's son, is owed my deepest gratitude for the time he spent getting all the data collated in his computer. His expertise was invaluable.

My thanks to Sheila Boudreaux for the time she spent turning all the information given to her into a manuscript.

Darlene McKnight spent many long hours transcribing audio cassettes and video tapes of Father's healing services. Thank you.

I would like to thank Doris Eisinger who also helped transcribe some of the audio tapes of the radio program.

Many thanks go to Gayle Ponseti, Merrill Martinez, and my husband, Harold for the time they spent in editing the manuscript.

I want to express my gratitude to Robert "Bob" Chauvin for his expertise and help. Thank you.

My undying gratitude goes to Mr. Edmond Joseph Orgeron, Jr. for allowing me to use his picture with Father for the cover.

My gratitude to Sonny Randon for the photograph we used for the cover.

v

Father Peter Mary Rookey, O.S.M.
Circa 1953

TABLE OF CONTENTS

A
TRIBUTE
TO

FATHER PETER MARY ROOKEY

FOR ALL HE HAS DONE
FOR
MARY'S HELPERS, INC

OUR LABOR OF LOVE

Father Peter Mary Rookey, O.S.M
Margaret M. Trosclair, S.O.S.M.

Tom Rookey, Bob Hope, Fr. Rookey, Dolores Hope

FATHER ROOKEY'S BIOGRAPHY

The following interview of Father Peter Mary Rookey, O.S.M. was recorded by Margaret Trosclair at her home on August 12, 1994, at 8:45 P.M.

(M) Father, I would like you to tell the folks about yourself, and all your family. Let's start with your family.

(F) Well, Margaret, my mother's name was Johanna McGarry. Ladies come first, right? So, I will start with her. She was one of twenty children from Stillwater, Minnesota. The state prison is located there, and my dad would tell her she would still be there if he hadn't bailed her out. Her family lived on a big farm outside the city. They had to have some way to feed all those mouths. My mother, whose father came to America from County Limerick, Ireland, was a teacher in the primary school in Stillwater. Once in America, he met a lady, Miss Byron, and married.

My father's name was Anthony Daniel Rookey, or, as he was called, A. D. Rookey. When we would pass the courthouse at home, we would see the initials A.D. 1924 on the cornerstone. As children, we thought those initials were my father's; however, the initials mean Anno Domini or Year of Our Lord. My dad's mother and father came from diverse backgrounds. His mother came to the United States from Ireland and met a Frenchman who had just come to America from France. His family name was Routhier, and her family name was Brady. I believe they met in New York or New York

1

Father Rookey's Parents
Anthony D. Rookey   Johanna McGarry Rookey

state. They married, and went across the St. Lawrence river to a place called Alexandria, which is near Cornwall, Ontario. My paternal grandparents, also, had a ranch, but only eleven mouths to feed as compared to my maternal side which had twenty to feed. For obvious reasons, all of the Routhier's, who moved down from Canada to the United States, changed their name to Rookey. It was difficult to spell, as well as pronounce for us Americans.

(M) Actually, your last name would have been Routhier not Rookey?

(F) Yes, the Routhier's, who moved to the United States, changed their name to Rookey. When I had the pleasure of meeting some of them, they would say our grandfathers were brothers, or we had the same grandparents, or something like that.

(M) Is there any more you can tell us about your parents?

(F) Yes, my dad was a logger in the timber and forest industry. After he became a logger, he came to Minnesota where he met my mother at an Irish Choeli, or dance. They fell in love, married, and moved from Stillwater to Willow River, Minnesota. Their first children, my oldest sister and brother, Rose and Chester, were born there. The four of them moved to Superior, Wisconsin where the other 11 were born. A total of 13 children.

My mother and father started a dray or hauling business. Using his horse and wagon, my father hauled oil for Standard Oil Company. Anyway, as children, we would take turns sitting on the front seat with our dad, and, if we were good, he would let us hold the reins of the

Serving the Forty-eight States

Rookey Transfer Company

horse. With the advent of the automobile, he acquired a truck or two, and went into the coal hauling business. Coal was a cheap commodity at that time, because the boats would bring the coal from the eastern United States. It would then be dumped on the docks of Lake Superior. From the docks, it would be hauled to the home.

My mother reared us from the office of the family business. Even though she was in charge of the office, she still had time to make the bread for our meals. Every once in a while, she would call home and tell us to punch down the bread, or to scrub the floors. She would come home three times a week, to bake twenty-five loaves of bread to feed her little army. At the office, she was behind the desk and on the phone. Even after we received a United Van Lines franchise, we still hauled coal. By the way, our telephone number was "9" and, in the early days, you only had one number because phones were very sparse. We advertised "Call 9" and one of the Rookey nine (we were 9 boys you see) will come and pick up your piano or whatever.

(M) Father, can you tell us about how your parents went to their eternal reward?

(F) My dad died in 1939 at the age of sixty-eight of a heart attack. He had retired some years before he died. My mother died of cancer at the age of seventy-three, and, during her illness, she died a number of deaths. When she would slip into unconsciousness, my brother would call me, and I would fly home. I would anoint her, give her the Sacrament of the Sick, and she'd come back to life! (Laughter) Another humorous incident happened when I was a young priest stationed in Portland, Oregon.

3

My oldest brother, Chester, who was the head of the family since our dad died, called to tell me mother was doing poorly. I immediately flew to Minneapolis where he met me, and we drove on to Superior. When we arrived at the hospital, she was unconscious, and appeared to be almost gone. I began translating from Latin the prayers for the people around the bed which included family members, and a couple of nuns. After I said, "Be merciful to your handmaid, Joan," she came out of it and said, "Johanna, dear." (Laughter) Another very funny thing happened during my mother's illness, and it had to do with a young, handsome Servite, Father Jim Quigley. He was a lovely character with a great sense of humor who overcame alcoholism. At one time, there were a lot of stories about how he used to duck his bottle under his pillow to keep the boys from knowing about it. After giving my mother the Last Rites, he was holding her hand while talking to her. He kept asking her if she knew him. "Do you know me, Mrs. Rookey?" "Do you know me, Mrs. Rookey?" Finally, she opened her eyes and said, "Father Quigley, how could I ever forget that handsome face of yours?" (Laughter)

(M) How could she forget? So, that got her out of it that time, too? (Laughter)

(F) On that same trip from Portland, she had all these tubes connected to her. She was diagnosed with abdominal or colon cancer. Because of not drinking enough liquids, as well as losing a lot of blood, she was dry as a bone. My mother never drank any alcohol, and there was never any alcohol in the house. Out of the blue, she starting yelling for a glass of beer. (Laughter) My brothers could not believe it. You know, it's been said that beer is good when you are "dry as a bone." (Laughter) Anyway, it

4

Johanna McGarry Rookey
"A Strong Willed Woman"

Father Rookey's Family ten of thirteen. Three not yet born. Top Row: Gordon, Rose, Mr. & Mrs. Rookey, Chester, Harold   Bottom Row: Genevieve, Kathryn, Peter, Bernard, Mary, Robert

was a Sunday night, and all the taverns were closed due to the Blue Laws. Chester, went all over town trying to cajole one of the "pub people" to open up and slip him a bottle. He finally found a willing man, and he bought a six pack or whatever it was at that time. There were only bottles in those days, no cans. Would you believe, that as he walked up the hospital steps, the bag tore, and all the bottles broke. (Laughter) In the meantime, her doctor, a handsome six foot six inch American Indian, who lived near the hospital went home, got a bottle of beer from his icebox, and brought it to her. (Laughter)

(M) It seems she was a very strong willed woman.
(F) Oh, that she was!

(M) I would imagine that the two of you must have laughed many times while reminiscing about those times.
(F) You know, to top that off, or to put the "frosting on the cake," she was given a few more years by the Lord. She died at the age of seventy-three which is great. Anyway, when she and the girls would get together to play cards, they would have a glass of beer. They were all in their seventies or more. I guess the doctor told her to drink a glass of beer.

(M) Father, tell us now about your brothers and sisters.
(F) Rose is the oldest. She is our matriarch who, if she lives, will be ninety-one years of age at Christmas time. I'm not sure of the date, but I do know her birthday is several days before Christmas. Rose married Martin Martinson, and they moved to California. They had one son. She is still in California; however, doing poorly at the moment. I don't know if she will live out the year.

5

Rookey Brothers
Top Row: Dick, Father Peter, Bob, Gordon
Bottom Row: Tom, Chester, Harold

Gordon & Velma Rookey
Bridesmaid Kathryn Rookey

Richard & Lola Rookey
Groomsmen: Brothers Earl, Bernard—Bridesmaid: Unknown

Emmett & Kathryn Rookey Connolly
Groomsman: Bill Murphy—Bridesmaid: Genevieve Rookey Stack

The next child was C. P., Chester Philip, and he became president of the family business. Chester waited until my mother died before marrying, because he took care of her until the end. He married Elizabeth Donnelly, who was of Scottish ancestry. They were both in their fifties when they married and did not have any children. Elizabeth, also, took care of her mother until she died. As a matter of fact, the two mothers died close together in dates and in time.

The third child was Gordon A. who married a Swedish convert by the name of Velma. They had four children.

The fourth child was Harold J. who married a lady from Duluth. I cannot remember her name. When you have so many, its very hard to recall. They had three children.

The fifth child was Mary. Mary was very loving, and she became kind of a second mother to us when Rose married and moved out west. She married a man by the name of Thompson who is deceased. They had a son who died as a child.

She, then, married Earl DeMara of Chicago, and lived there for some years. They had one daughter, Marilyn, who became well known in Illinois. She was a teacher at Loyola University of Chicago, where, I believe she taught Political Science. Marilyn married a man by the name of Bill Clancy. I use to call him and tell him he must have arrived on the first of the month with the rest of the bills (an old gag). They both did very well financially. They have four children, and they live in Oak Park, Illinois in one of the buildings of the famous architect, Harold Wright. Marilyn is called "Dee" because of her fathers name, DeMara, which is Belgian. When she ran for Congress, she made the mistake of running against a household name, Hyde. He is a Republican from Oak Park who is very popular. His amendment, the Hyde Amendment, is pro-life. Dee ran on the Democrat ticket, and she didn't have a "tinkers chance," even though she received 40% of the vote. My sister, Mary, died in Superior, Wisconsin at the age of 32 from cancer of the uterus.

The next one was Robert J. Rookey. He was a great youth leader.

(M) Is that your sixth brother you're talking about?
(F) Yes, he married a Swedish girl, Vera. In 1990, Robert was killed instantly in a head-on automobile collision just outside Superior. Vera has also passed away. As I mentioned earlier, he was great with youth clubs, baseball teams and all that sort of thing. Robert and Vera had four children. Their youngest son, Tim, is a treasury of information about the family. He is a family tree buff who lives in Madison, Wisconsin.

(M) Didn't I meet Tim?
(F) Yes, you met Tim Rookey. He's a brilliant lad, and has a very good position with the state government in Madison, Wisconsin. He recently married, and as yet has no children.

The next one is Genevieve. She became a nurse, and worked as one in an ammunition plant, as well as in hospitals. Genevieve married Joseph Stack, and had four children. Margaret, you met Joseph at my Golden Jubilee celebration in 1991.

7

Bernard Rookey
World War II

The eighth one is Kathryn. She married Emmett Connolly, and they had nine children. Kathryn and Emmett tragically lost two babies. I believe one smothered, and the other was killed in an accident. Emmett died, and she married John Madigan, who was a professor at St. Thomas College in St. Paul, Minnesota. Seminarians go to St. Thomas College while studying for the priesthood, so John knew many priests. John was a very fine gentleman who died about two years after they were married. Kathryn is a double widow, and still lives in Minneapolis.

Then myself.

(M) You were number nine?
(F) Yes, I was born October 12, 1916.

(M) Number ten?
(F) Number ten is Bernard. He is married to Lois, and they have one child, Bernard or Bernie. Lois and Bernard live in Mesa, Arizona which is near Phoenix.

The next one, number eleven, is Dale. Dale was a handsome young fellow who joined the Air Force at nineteen. He was about to get his wings when he died from an appendectomy in January, 1942 at Scott Air Force Base in Texas. His death made my mother the first Gold Star Mother in Wisconsin. Roosevelt declared war on the eve of the Immaculate Conception, 1941. It occurred the very same year I was ordained.

Thomas Earl is number twelve. Actually, his name is Earl Thomas, but they all called him Tom. He married Rita O'Toole from Duluth, Minnesota, who died in 1994.

They moved from Long Beach, California to a little place in Nevada on the California border. Her death was sudden. She died of cancer in about a week's time. They had five children, two girls and three boys.

The final one, number thirteen, is Richard J. He is the only family member still living in our hometown, Superior, Wisconsin. Lola, his wife, died quite a number of years ago. Richard and Lola had three children, two boys and a girl.

(M) Now, let's now go back to when you were born.

(F) As mentioned previously, I was born October 12, 1916, at 1210 Ogden Avenue, in Superior, Wisconsin. I guess you would say I was a war baby. World War I was going on, and my brother would ask, jokingly, where was the war when I broke out. The house where I was born was destroyed and the local newspaper, "The Telegram," built a handsome building there. The house I remember the most was a three story one that has since been turned into three apartments. I grew up in that house which was located at 1617 Ogden Avenue. I was just a little kid, but I can remember carrying some of the things from the old house up the street to the new one. We were not a wealthy family; however, we always had enough to eat and always had clean clothes to wear. In fact, my mother's favorite expression was "Cleanliness is next to Godliness." I'm sure you heard that many times.

(M) Yes!

(F) We were dressed in hand-me-downs, which is not unusual for large families. My dad was an upright man who was the cool one in the family. On the other hand, my mother was the feisty one, and she did most of the "ruling of the roost." She had a good head, a heart of gold, and was very generous. She always had her Sunday envelope for the church, and taught us to be generous. My dad worked hard, and the boys helped him. At the tender age of thirteen, when I saw work on the horizon, I pulled out and went to the seminary.

(M) Father, before that, I understand you were blind. What age was that? Was it an accident?

(F) Yes, it was an accident. I think I was seven years old, but I'm not sure anymore. It was so long ago. My brother and I were fooling around with a great big firecracker that wouldn't go off. We blew on it. It exploded right in our faces and it destroyed my eyes.

(M) You say you were blind. How long were you blind?

(F) Well it seemed like an eternity. Of course, when you're in the dark, it is not pleasant.

(M) Would you say a year?

(F) I would say less than a year.

(M) You know what it's like to be blind. How was your sight restored?

(F) Just by prayer.

(M) Just by prayer. Did someone pray over you?

(F) We just prayed. They didn't know about laying of hands on people at the time. We just prayed, especially the Rosary. Dr. Barnsdahl, an eye, ear, nose and throat

10

specialist, lived just a few doors down the street, and they brought me to him. He said he could do nothing to help me, except to change the bandages. It was actually just prayers that brought my eyesight back.

(M) Father, I would like to know, if you can still remember, what were your feelings at that time? I'm sure, even as a child, you must have been devastated.

(F) I was completely devastated and frightened. When you lose your sight, you lose a lot. Anyway, this is the way I would describe it. You can say that my blindness made me pray very hard.

(M) Would you say this brought your family of thirteen children closer together? Were they very religious before your accident?

(F) Well, my mother always reared us in the fear and the love of God. Yes, they were religious, and I think this helped us pray together as a family.

(M) Did your sight return gradually, or was it instantly?

(F) At first it was gradual with little glimmers of light. As time progressed, the pieces came back together leaving the muscles of my eye lids very weak. I had to exercise them constantly to make them strong again.

(M) I see you now without glasses. Did you ever have to wear them?

(F) I only acquired glasses late in my studies, because I was able to read my books without them. I can still read a telephone book without glasses; however, when I read for any length of time, my eyes get tired and I will use them.

(M) You entered the seminary at the age of thirteen. Was it a gradual desire that started with your time as an altar boy?

(F) No, I was never an altar boy, but I went to devotions often.

(M) Did you go to devotions on your own, or did your mother bring you?

(F) No, I went on my own.

(M) Did you, as well as your brothers and sisters, attend Catholic school?

(F) We all did. As a child, I would conduct May Devotions in our home which consisted of saying the Rosary.

(M) Father, tell us about the time when you told your family about your desire to enter the seminary.

(F) I was in the eighth grade when I told my mother I wanted to be a priest. I believe she was praying for this for a long time, because she was not surprised. We had some Servites at St. Patrick's Church in Superior, and quite a number of young boys were going to the Servites at that time.

In 1930, I entered the Servite Seminary located in Hillside, Illinois which is a suburb of Chicago. For our recreation, we would walk through the cemetery. Queen of Heaven Cemetery is located in Hillside where the alleged apparitions of Jesus and Mary are taking place right now. In fact, Our Lady allegedly appears there to an octogenarian, Joe Reinholtz. He and I are very close. In fact, we belong to the same prayer group which meets every Wednesday at New Deluxe Bakery, 4242 South Archer Street, Chicago, Illinois.

Father Rookey & Harold Trosclair

(M) Father, were you about to say something else?

(F) Yes. The seminary, in its early years, was called Mater Dolorosa Seminary. They changed the name to Servite, because Mater Dolorosa is a mouth full for most people. By the way, Mater Dolorosa means Mother of Sorrows. We have a beautiful chapel inside the seminary. I celebrated my first Mass, and was the Sacristan there. When Ivan, the Medjugorje visionary, visited Chicago about four years ago, he had a visitation from the Blessed Mother in the chapel. (Oh! Oh! here comes the big gun (Harold), we're not on tape right now are we?)

(M) Yes, we are Father.

(F) You're on tape, Harold. I'm glad you are on tape because you are part of this.

(M) Harold treats you well, Father, serving you banana splits. I know this is the highlight of your day.

(F) This is enough for all three of us. We'll have to have a little taste.

(Harold) I gave you more because you worked the hardest!! (Laughter)

(M) The ice cream at the Trosclair's is the highlight of your visit. I thought it was the healing services and the good friends. (Laughter)

(F) Let's see. Yes, back to my seminary years. I was ordained in the Basilica of Our Lady of Sorrows in 1941. Archbishop John O'Brien ordained my class of seven; however, only three are still living. After the Archbishop ordains you, in the first part of the ordination Mass, you then con-celebrate with the Archbishop the remainder of the Mass. This is the first time you say, "This is My Body, This is My Blood" with the ordaining bishop. The

Father Rookey's first Mass in hometown Superior, Wisconsin
May, 1941

first Mass I celebrated on my own was in the Chapel of Mater Dolorosa Seminary where I also made my solemn vows.

(M) Father, through your seminary years, is there anything significant that stands out in your mind?

(F) I know I was tempted to leave. Like a person's faith, if it's worth anything, it has to be tested. I have Father Raymond Mary Couglin, O.S.M. and Father James Mary Keane, O.S.M. to thank for their counseling and encouragement. They told me this was probably just a severe temptation.

(M) Father, when you said your first official Mass, how did you feel?

(F) Oh! I just felt so humbled. I just felt those words "I am not worthy Lord, I am not worthy Lord" so powerfully. My mother and some of the family were there at that Mass.

(M) I know they were very proud that day.

(F) Of course, they were. According to my brother Chester, a funny thing happened the day of my ordination. (Laughter) Chester and some buddies drove down from Superior to Chicago. One of his buddies was a fellow by the name of Johnson who was all banged up from a recent accident. He was severely injured, and he eventually died from the effects of the accident. My brother brought along another friend to distract Johnson. Johnson, by the way, was not Catholic. The Ordination Mass was a little longer than the usual Mass. My brother had to get Johnson back to the motel to have his bandages changed. When they arrived at the motel, there was no place to park. Chester pulled into a "No Parking" spot near the door of the motel. A big Irish cop came over and said (with an Irish brogue), "You can't park here"!! Then, he saw Johnson with all his bandages and said, "What's your name?" Johnson replied, "McCarthy, Sir." Well, he said, "You can park for ten minutes." (Laughter) A little lie.

(M) He hadn't heard about sending your angel ahead of you to find a parking place, did he? Send your Angel ahead and you'll have a parking place!

(F) Talking about Angels has triggered my memory to tell you this story. On Tuesday, August 9, 1994, we had an outdoor Mass at the home of our attorney, John Krupa. He and his wife have been very much touched by the Lord. While we celebrated Mass in their garden, John's wife and another lady saw Our Blessed Mother above the altar. The other lady, who is very gifted spiritually, said there were angels all around the altar and two big angels on either side with swords. I guess they were there to ward off any evil. It's time for a funny story. A boy goes to his confessor and the priest says, "Anything else, Sonny Boy?" The boy replied, "Oh, yes, I have other sins but I'm saving those for next time." (Laughter) No use over doing, right?

(M) Father tell us about your ministry after you were ordained?

(F) In 1948, after several assignments, I was assigned to assist Father James Mary Keane, O.S.M. who founded the College of Our Lady of Benburb in Northern Ireland. After he started the ball rolling, he was transferred, and went on to other great work in other countries. I was appointed to take over this new foundation of the Servites in Ireland.

(M) You took over as pastor?

(F) There's not a parish there. It's a large complex place. It is a center where we have retreats, as well as all kind of devotions, and activities for the youths. They handle forty thousand youths there every year. In the beginning, we had to struggle to survive. We had only a couple of newly ordained priests, and we had to get a faculty for the college to teach our seminarians. Then, I had to teach, give retreats, get known, preach missions, as well as many other duties. Eventually, I had to slow down to a "waltz," because I became anemic. It took me years to get over this, and get my strength back. After a short stay in the hospital, I went to stay with a dear friend, Monsignor Tohall in Louth, County Louth.

(M) Was it like a nervous breakdown?

(F) It was more like a general wearing out, because you can't operate at full speed. You need to slow down and gather your strength again.

In June 1953, I was elected to the office of Assistant General of the Servite Order in Rome. This assignment helped a lot, because it was a slower pace. I traveled to Servite installations in Belgium, Ireland, Lapland, Africa, and the Middle East.

After finishing a six year term as Assistant General of the Servites in Rome, I was then asked, in June, 1959, to head up our Servite International College in Louvain, Belgium. (The famous television and radio star, Bishop Fulton Sheen, graduated from the University.) Directing young and future priests in the languages of French, Spanish, Italian, and English, made this the most difficult assignment. In the summer of 1962, I was assigned, as an assistant, to the Basilica of Our Lady of Sorrows, a Servite Parish, in Chicago, Illinois. In the spring of 1963, Most Rev. Fr. Alphonse Mary Monta, Prior General of the Order of Servites, asked me to help the Order in Germany. I helped train novices at the Shrine of Our Lady in Weinlinden, south of Munich. I studied German at the Sprachinstitut, Walchensee near Garmisch-Partenkirchen, Ettal Abtei and Mittenwald where the famous Stradivarius violins are made. In 1964, Father Amadeus Maria Schmacher, the Servite Provincial, assigned me to the Holy Cross Servite Priory and Church in Dusseldorf, Germany, and then to Assumption Priory and Church in Gelsenkirchen-Buer, Germany which are both in the Rhineland region.

In 1968, Fr. Terrence Mary O'Connor, our Chicago Provincial, brought me back to the United States. He assigned me to the missions in the Ozarks. We served in many counties, a very large area, with few Catholics. We served Most Rev. Archbishop Ignatius Strecker, His Eminence Cardinal William Baum, and His Eminence Cardinal Bernard Law until 1985.

In 1985 I was assigned to Our Lady of Sorrows Basilica, in Chicago. I was encouraged by my superiors, Fr. Augustine Mary Kulbis and Fr. Michael Mary Doyle, to begin the healing ministry, "The International Compassion Ministry," named after Our Mother of Sorrows. "The obedient man shall speak of victory." We began with services on the First Saturday of every month in our Basilica. Mary told us, in Fatima, to consecrate the first Saturdays to her with Reconciliation

Father Rookey's Golden Jubilee Celebration—May, 1991
L/R Fr. Dominic Mary Manzo, Fr. Peter Mary Rookey, Fr. Philip Mary Brennan

(confession), Mass, Communion and the mysteries of the Rosary. With God's help, we have had a First Saturday Mass and healing service ever since. We have services over a good part of the globe, but we always return for First Saturday. Jesus and Mary appear every First Saturday in the Basilica and are seen by large crowds.

(M) Thank you, Father. What a beautiful life dedicated to God's service. I know you have been a priest for 55 years, and you had a lovely Golden Jubilee celebration.

(F) Yes, Margaret. On May 26, 1991, at the Basilica of Our Lady of Sorrows, I, along with Fr. Philip Mary Brennan and Fr. Dominic Mary Manzo, celebrated fifty years as a priest and a Servant of Mary. We were seven in our class ordained fifty years before, and today we have three left. It was a joyous day surrounded by family, friends, and, I remember, you were there also.

(M) Yes, Father it was a great day to remember.

(F) That it was! Just like today, a beautiful day to remember.

Our Lady of Lourdes of Medjugorje

ENTHRONEMENT OF OUR LADY OF LOURDES OF MEDJUGORJE STATUE

The following is a partial transcript from a radio show taped on October 9, 1988 with Father Peter Mary Rookey, O.S.M. and Margaret Trosclair.

(M) Good morning. I'm Margaret Trosclair on station WSMB-AM, and I want to welcome all of you to "Reports of Medjugorje." I would like to begin with the Lord's Prayer. "Our Father, Who art in heaven, hallowed be Thy Name; Thy kingdom come; Thy Will be done on earth, as it is in heaven. Give us this day our daily bread; and forgive us our trespasses, as we forgive those who trespass against us; and lead us not into temptation; but deliver us from evil. Amen."

This morning we have a very special guest, Father Peter Mary Rookey, O.S.M. who is from Chicago. We are doing this show live from the studio, and Father and Cathy McCarthy are at the airport. They are leaving today for Medjugorje. In fact, they will be boarding their plane at 12:30 P.M. for New York, and, then, for Medjugorje. Cathy was here for the celebration that took place at The Visitation of Our Lady Parish in Marrero, Louisiana. We are waiting for Father Rookey to telephone us from the airport. I believe he is on the phone now. Good Morning, Father Rookey.

(F) Hello! Is this Margaret? God bless you, Margaret.

(M) "God bless you, Father." I would like to tell you a little bit about Father Rookey . He is stationed at St. Dominic

Church in Chicago, and he has been with us at Visitation since Wednesday night helping us have a wonderful celebration in honor of the enthronement of the replica statue of Our Lady of Lourdes of Medjugorje. It is a pleasure to have Father on the telephone. He is a Servite priest who carries a cross with relics of the Seven Holy Founders and all the Servite saints. I am going to let him tell you about the celebration. "It is my pleasure to have you here, today on WSMB Radio, and the audience is very excited about your being on the air. It is a thrill for me to have you here."

(F) Margaret, this is my seventh trip to Medjugorje, and I will be leaving from J.F.K. Airport. Cathy and I are at the New Orleans airport waiting to leave. I was so honored to have been invited by you and the parish of The Visitation of Our Lady in Marrero. I was delighted throughout the celebration, and I want to share with our listeners the powerful graces that came as a result of the presence of the thousands who came to pray to the Lord through Our Lady of Lourdes of Medjugorje. The results were very apparent during the healing service and the beautiful procession. All of the events of the celebration were overwhelming. I think we were treated to the 'oil of gladness' by the Holy Spirit. We were all filled with His gladness. Margaret, you are a wonderful instrument of the Lord.

(M) Thank you, Father.

(F) I just don't know how to thank you, as well as all of Mary's Helpers, who are responsible for listening and carrying out God's Word. I am a Servite Priest, Servants of Mary, founded by seven young lay persons like Margaret and her husband, Harold, and all of Mary's Helpers who are lay people. In 1233, we were founded

20

by seven young men, most of them married, and born in Italy during the time of Francis and Dominic. I think my mission in the world is to share with everyone the charism of Mary. We back up the words of the Lord as He backed up His own Words. "Believe My Words," He said. He backs up His Words with the miracles that follow. We've seen miracles from all over the world, and miracles do follow His Words. His Words and His power are shown so strongly in Medjugorje through His Blessed Mother. There are healing services often in Medjugorje, and, now, as we go over there this week, I am sure the Lord will work many more wonders as He has in the past. I don't want to speak too long, because I know you, Margaret, have a lot to say, also.

(M) I would like to share with all the faithful and the wonderful listeners, who were not at the celebration, the wonderful blessings we shared. Maybe, a little healing touch is what we really need for the listeners. So many of them cry out in pain, that, maybe this can console them, and, from this, they would know that God is with them. I'm going to let you do that now.

(F) I would like to share with our listeners a prayer we usually pray when we lay on hands, and ask the Lord to heal them, the **Miracle Prayer**. I am going to pray this with all our listeners. Often the healing takes place through the media, such as the radio or telephone. The Lord has healed people through telephone calls from Ireland, as well as many other places. His power is not contained by time or space, nor are His blessings. The Centurion, in the Gospel, asks Our Lord to heal his servant who was at death's door. Jesus said, "I will come and heal him." The Centurion replied, "Oh Lord, You do not have to do that, You're just like I am. I send the message and my servants do my will. I am sure You can do the same. I am not worthy that You should come under my roof, just say the word and my servant will be healed." That's what happened, and, at the very moment, the servant was healed. We can be healed right now if we wish; therefore, open yourself to the Lord and His healing.

(M) Father, before you begin, I would like you to tell the listeners about our skeptic, Father Maughan, who is no longer a skeptic.

(F) We came to The Visitation of Our Lady Church in Marrero, Louisiana for the enthronement of Our Lady of Lourdes of Medjugorje statue. We were very touched when we were able to participate in the celebration of Benediction with Archbishop Philip N. Hannan, who is a very holy and dedicated man. There are always doubts at a healing service whether anything will happen. The doubts were laid to rest on the first evening when we had the healing service for some of the handicapped who could not attend the service on Friday evening. It was at this service that Father Maughan witnessed a man, who was in a wheelchair, walk out of the church pushing his wheelchair. Praise God! Give Him all the glory. "Not to us, O Lord, but to Your Name be the glory." I have a confirmation concerning a young man who was healed over the air . Larry Riemer, who is standing next to me now, stood in for a friend who was in a coma. His friend received a healing at that moment, and came out of the coma. Praise God! So many other healings like that come about just like that one. I remember my brother Servite, Father Martin Mary Jenko, who was held captive in Beirut for eighteen months, and then released. Oh, what a beautiful man! I had him as a student in Rome.

His nephew, twenty-two years of age, was in a coma for a long time as a result of an accident at work. We prayed, and he came out of the coma. He is now leading a normal life, except for some eye trouble. Praise God, and give Him all the glory! I would like to emphasize the power in Medjugorje, because there we see so many miraculous happenings, such as the 'miracle of the sun.' In our daily lives, there are healings galore. It is such a great grace to go to Medjugorje. The Lord enriches the ministry every time I go there. In Chicago, every First Saturday at 11:00 A.M., we have a healing service, and you can have someone stand in for you. Margaret, we will give you the details and the phone number.

(M) Father, I would like to tell the listeners one more story before you start the **Miracle Prayer**. On the day I left to hitchhike from Medjugorje to Italy, you held a healing service in the graveyard in Medjugorje. You know the one I'm talking about. Father Ives helped you in that healing service, and I would like you to tell that story.

(F) Is that the one about the exorcism?

(M) Yes.

(F) This happened on the seventh anniversary of the apparitions, June 25, 1988. It seems Our Lady wants us to witness more wonderful things for Her anniversary. A young man, twenty-nine years of age, from Australia came to us, and told us he had the feeling he was possessed. As he came up to be blessed, it became obvious that his feeling was correct. The demon made him rise and foam. The young man wanted out, but the demon didn't want out. He began to spit and vomit on me, and luckily we had more than a half dozen priests who had come for a blessing that could help. They saw what was happening, and they added their priestly presence to the exorcism. One of the priests was Father Ives Aniban, of St. Anthony Church in Gretna, Louisiana, who was assisting me. I tried to get this young man to say "Jesus is Lord." Of course, he could not say it. St. Paul assures us that no one can say "Jesus is Lord," except through the power of the Holy Spirit. That is a perfect way for someone to know if there is a presence of the demonic. I asked for some holy water. Someone had some water from Lourdes, and I sprinkled some of it on the young man. The demon yelled and screamed to high heaven. He is a coward, but somehow I did not feel frightened even though some people did have to leave because of the exorcism. Then, he started barking like a dog while having another one of his tantrums. It just so happened there was a dog behind me. I said in one last gesture, "Since you won't give us your name, you must be legion, you must be many, but it does not matter. Jesus knows you. You've been barking like a dog, so in the Name of Jesus I command you to go inside this dog, right now, at this very moment." And, by gosh, he did. He was finally delivered, and he 'rested in the Spirit.' He was able to say, "In the Name of Jesus, and Jesus is Lord." Praise God! I am reminded of an interview I had with Padre Pio. I was able to talk to him several times while I was stationed in Italy for six years. A man who was very close to him spoke about demons in the world. He said Padre Pio had mentioned that there are more demons attacking us in the world than there are people that have been born from the beginning of the world until now. But, and this is encouraging, there are many, many more angels protecting us from them.

(M) Unfortunately, we have little time left. Why don't you start, Father, the **Miracle Prayer**.

(F) I will do that right now. "Praise You, Jesus." Spirit of the living God, fall afresh on all that are listening here and all that are standing in for someone. Spirit of the living God, just fall afresh on them. You said "All power is given to Me in heaven and on earth. Preach the gospel, to all nations baptizing them in the Name of the Father, and of the Son, and of the Holy Spirit. Those who believe, and are baptized will be saved. For those who believe, these signs will follow. In My Name, they will cast out demons. The sick, upon whom they lay their hands, will recover." Jesus, we are encouraged by Your Words, and we do as You say. First, we want to cleanse ourselves of all obstacles to our healing, mainly any unforgiveness, or pride. "We humble ourselves before You a humble and contrite heart, O Lord, You will not despise. We bow ourselves before You, Jesus. You are God and Savior." All of you who are in our listening audience, would you like to pray with me the **Miracle Prayer**? As we pray this prayer, there is something very wonderful that is going to happen to us, so pray with us. It is good to look at a Crucifix while saying this prayer. If you can pray very loudly, do so, and this will give you courage. Are you ready? Repeat after me.

MIRACLE PRAYER

Lord Jesus, - I come before You, just as I am. - I am sorry for my sins, - I repent of my sins, - please forgive me. - In Your Name - I forgive all others - for what they have done against me. - I renounce satan, - the evil spirits and all their works. - I give You my entire self, Lord Jesus - now and forever. - I invite You into my life, Lord Jesus, - I accept You as my Lord, God and Savior. - Heal me, change me, - strengthen me in body, soul and spirit. Come Lord Jesus, - cover me with Your Precious Blood and fill me with Your Holy Spirit. - I love You Lord Jesus, - I praise You, Jesus. - I thank You Jesus. - I shall follow You every day of my life. - Amen.- Mary my mother, - Queen of Peace, - all the angels and saints, - please help me. - Amen.

(M) That was wonderful, Father, and I would like to take this opportunity to thank you for the wonderful healings that God has worked through you.

(F) Thank you, Margaret. Remember, we will be bringing all those petitions to Medjugorje. God bless you, Gayle, and all of Mary's Helpers.

The following testimonies resulted from the radio program and the healing service on the welcoming celebration weekend.

At one time, I suffered from deterioration of the bones in my spine which caused me to be hunched over. I suffered from this for seventeen years. Before this condition arose, I was five feet, seven inches, but, as the hump in my back developed, I was down to four feet, eleven inches. I couldn't walk, or get up, without help. Leaning back in a chair wasn't possible nor was sitting up straight. Every day, I prayed for a healing.

On October 9, 1988, I heard Father Rookey praying the **Miracle Prayer** over the radio. I prayed along with him, and asked God to take away the pain I was experiencing. I began to feel funny. It was like I was being lifted or drawn into another world, and this sensation frightened me.

I began to feel well. The lump in my back disappeared, and I could, once again, lean back in a chair. I stood up straight and walked without holding on to anything. I could even dance again. When I went to church for the first time since my healing, I was drunk with happiness.

I thank Jesus every day for my healing, and I also thank Margaret Trosclair and Mary's Helpers for bringing Father Rookey here.

Almita Peters

I have a pinched Sciatic nerve in my spine, and when it is inflamed, the pain is more than I can bear. In fact, it is so bad sometimes that I sob out loud. I cannot dress myself without help. The pain starts in my lower back, like a lightning rod, shoots to my hips, and down to my heels and insteps. Because I take inflammation medicine, I couldn't take anything for the pain except Tylenol.

I always have had great faith, and I prayed daily to be healed. My husband, who has heart trouble, and I heard Father Rookey pray the **Miracle Prayer** for healing on the WSMB Radio program. While we listened to Father say the **Miracle Prayer**, my husband put his hand on my back, and I placed my hand on his heart. The shooting pains in my back, legs and feet are gone. I can lift my feet, and dress myself without help. My husband's heart condition has not worsened.

Irma Phillpott

On October 4, 1988, after Dr. Robert Carter reviewed the results of the CAT Scan of my left lung, I had an appointment with him to discuss the outcome. He told me he was eighty-nine percent sure I had cancer, and, if I were to wait a year, it would be too late for surgery. I agreed to have the surgery the following Tuesday.

I attended a healing service at The Visitation of Our Lady Church in Marrero, Louisiana on October 6, 1988. After the evening Mass, the service began. It was conducted by Father Peter Mary Rookey of Chicago, Illinois. The replica statue was unveiled during the Mass. I walked to the front of the church, and stood by the altar close to the new statue of Mary. While I waited for Father to pray over me, I kept looking directly at the Blessed Mother. When Father reached me, he blessed me. It was as if I had lost control of my body and fell backwards. I had the feeling I had been healed. I knew, at that moment, when it came time for surgery, the doctor wouldn't find any trace of cancer.

I was admitted to West Jefferson Medical Center on Sunday, October 9, 1988. On Monday, the orderly came to get me to take a chest X-ray. I told the orderly the doctor wasn't going to find anything wrong. He said he hoped I was right.

On Tuesday, after surgery, Dr. Carter went into the waiting room and gave the results to my family and friends. Entering the room with a puzzled look on his face, he told everyone the surgery went well. There was no cancer, only a fungus on the outside of one of my lungs.

When he discharged me from the hospital, I told him what happened at the healing service, and showed him a statue of the Blessed Mother. He said it was good to have faith. I believed in prayer before, but since my healing, my belief is stronger than ever.

Dorothy Solanka

For twenty years, I have suffered from severe migraine headaches. Because I was on heavy medication from the doctor, I never went anywhere without my pain pills. Sometimes the headaches lasted for three days at a time, and I would have to take as many as five strong pills to get relief. Never more than one week would go by, sometimes less, before I would feel the onset of another headache. In October, when Father Rookey was here for the presentation of the statue at The Visitation of Our Lady Church, he was a guest on the radio show, "Reports of Medjugorje." He said the **Miracle Prayer** over the radio, adding that anyone saying the prayer with him could be healed by Jesus, even though the prayer was on tape. One day, after suffering a three day long migraine, as well as being depressed, I decided to ask Jesus for help. I had never asked Him before, because I thought others had worse illnesses that needed to be cured. At the time, I was disgusted and sick. I put Father Rookey's tape on, and prostrated myself before my altar at home. I prayed the prayer in a manner I heard Father Cohen say it on his television show. Father Rookey's voice said "pray, beg, and thank Him" all at one time. I did just that "Jesus," I said, "Please take these headaches away from me, I can't stand them anymore. I beg you, Jesus, and I thank you." After I finished praying, I still had the headache, but I felt healed. The next day the headache was gone. I haven't had one since, and that has been two months. Sometimes, I feel the pain approaching, but its as though a shield is in front of me, not letting the pain in. I think it is the Precious Blood of

Jesus that is completely covering me, and shielding me. I have hesitated about giving my testimony, but yesterday I heard Margaret Trosclair say over the radio that satan is right there to tempt us not to believe, even to the point of feeling that the pain is coming back. She said not to be afraid to believe that Jesus heals us. Margaret gave me the strength to write my testimony, because twice satan did just that. I felt a slight headache coming on, and I started believing that I wasn't healed. I took regular Anacin, and it went away. I am really healed, and the shield protects me. I thank and praise Jesus every day for this healing, and for sending us Father Rookey, a true disciple of Jesus.

Cecile Panepinto

I went to the healing service to ask for a conversion, but, while waiting in line for Father Rookey's blessing, I was asked to stand in for Sharon Murphy, who was in the hospital. I closed my eyes, and remembered the May crowning when I was a child. I had been chosen to crown the Blessed Mother. What an honor to be chosen again, but this time for Sharon, who now lay in God's grace. With my eyes closed, I envisioned Mary standing above me with Jesus beside her. I reached up to Her, and She reached down to me. I felt touched as Father Rookey bestowed a short blessing. "Should I leave now," I wondered. Again, I envisioned Mary, and I reached out my hands to Her. This time, as She reached toward me, She was half bent between me and Jesus, Who was carrying His Cross. Sharon was trying to walk behind Mary, but kept slipping on Jesus' blood. Mary said to me, "See what sin has done to beautiful Sharon, and what it has done to my Son." I then envisioned Jesus and Mary standing by Sharon's bed as Father Rookey prayed over me, and I, almost immediately, went down, resting in the Spirit. Sharon's beautiful spirit rose joyfully, and reached out to Mary as I rested.

Stella Barnes

Because of nine operations, I suffer from massive scar tissue which limits my daily activities. If I over extend myself one day, I needed total bed rest the next day. On October 7, 1988, I was determined to participate in the procession for Our Lady. Neither my mother, nor my children wanted me to do that much walking. Knowing I would be late, I had my daughter bring me to the starting point. I was not concerned how I would get home. When I arrived, I was five minutes late. I had to run about a quarter of a mile to catch up with everyone. When I reached the group, I was tired, and out of breath. I continued the two mile walk from St. John Bosco Church in Harvey to Visitation of Our Lady Church in Marrero. As I walked, I felt no pain. I felt I was floating on air, and being pushed forward by an unknown force. As I sat in church listening to Father Rookey, I could feel the awful pain in my side returning. After Mass, I remained in church for the healing service. During the service, I turned, and saw my mother standing there. I was no longer concerned about my ride home. When Father Rookey prayed over me, I could feel the Holy Spirit flowing through me. After the service, I went home, and went to bed. By this time, the pain was so terrible, I had tears in my eyes. The tears were not just tears of pain, but of sorrow, also. I knew I would not be able to return to Visitation for the service in the morning. On October 8, 1988, I woke up with no pain. I got up, dressed myself, and returned to Visitation. I am praying, and standing in proxy for others. I do this for those who cannot attend the services in order that they may receive the same spiritual and physical healings that I received from God through Father Rookey.

Patricia Jackson

Several years ago I was attending 8:45 A.M. Mass at The Visitation of Our Lady Church in Marrero, and to my delight the celebrant was Father Rookey.

Because of tendinitis, I was suffering with a great deal of pain in both of my arms. I could no longer lift a gallon of milk, remove lids from jars, or perform many other duties a housewife normally performs in a day. Every task was a monumental one. I had been to the doctors, and had been given cortisone injections. However, I was still in a great deal of pain.

After Mass, I waited for Father Rookey. When I met him, I said, "Please, Fr. Rookey, pray for me. I have tendinitis in both of my arms." Father Rookey held both of my arms in his hands and prayed. He put his hand on top of my head, and prayed some more. I thanked him, and went about my daily duties. As time went by, I realized my arms were free of pain. To this day, I have not suffered with tendinitis.

Father Rookey is a kind, gentle, loving, spiritual soul. He is truly a man of God.

Jenelle Davis

REFLECTIONS ON MESSAGES FROM MEDJUGORJE

The following conversation is an excerpt from the April 9, 1989 interview between Father Peter Mary Rookey, O.S.M., Father Joe Benson, and Margaret Trosclair of WSMB Radio in New Orleans.

(M) We had the pleasure this week of receiving a telephone call from Father Joe Benson of St. Edward Church in Metairie. He had surgery on his back a week ago, and he experienced a beautiful healing. I have Father Benson on the hotline right now. Good Morning, Father.

(FB) Good Morning, Margaret.

(M) Father, while we are talking to Father Rookey, I would like you to tell us what happened to you in Belfast and in New Orleans.

(FB) Margaret, as you, and a lot of the people listening know, I'm described as a F.B.I. which means, Full Blooded Irishman.

(FR) I thought it meant Foreign Born Irish!

(FB) I came from the city of Belfast in Northern Ireland. Just over three weeks ago, I was talking to one of my aunts in Belfast. During the conversation, she told me about Father Rookey. I told my aunt that I had heard of you, because I remembered you had been here in October. She told me, that at one of the healing services held at St. Anne's, on the outskirts of Belfast, a lady came forward with a child, and you prayed with the two of them.

(FR) It was a Down's syndrome child, Right?

(FB) Yes, that's right. You prayed with them and they returned to the congregation. Some time later, during the service, you asked one of the ushers to go down and get her, and have her come up. She came up with the child, and she began to tell her story. She, in fact, had given birth to twins. One of the babies died, and the child who lived was Mongoloid. You prayed with the child. After praying with him, I believe it was a boy, I'm not sure, you said to her, "Nothing might happen just right now, but within two or three weeks you should see something." A few weeks later the child was sitting on his grandma's knee, and he went into what they thought were convulsions. Then, he jumped down from her knee, walked across the room for the first time in his life, turned and asked for "mama."

(FR) Praise the Lord, that's beautiful!

(FB) My aunt told me that story, and that was fine. I made a note of it, because I was impressed with God's work. A few days later, I reached a stage where I was in a lot of pain. A friend of mine tried to make contact with you. At about 7:30 P.M. on a Friday you called.

(FR) It was St. Patrick's Feast Day, March 17, 1989 I remember it well. What better day is there to talk to an Irishman from Belfast right from County Down where St. Patrick is seven feet down in Downpatrick.

(FB) Could you ask for anything more? You called, and we prayed together. The significant thing was that while we were praying, one of the orthopedic surgeons called to find out about my condition. I wasn't expecting him to call. His immediate response to the situation, when he heard that I was being prayed with by a priest over the phone was, "Okay, I'm not going to interrupt that. What I'll do is call back every ten minutes until Father is finished praying. I just want to see how's he doing?" It was very, very clear to me that this was the man I wanted to perform the surgery on me. That was Friday. On Sunday, I called my aunt, and told her I managed to get in touch with you, or rather, you had contacted me. The really surprising thing was that she had spent all that day, St. Patrick's Day, in Ireland, praying and fasting that somehow, some way, Father Rookey would be able to get in touch with me.

(M) Praise God! Just give glory and praise to God!

(FR) That testimony is just another proof that Ireland is the land of saints and scholars.

(FB) I missed out on both, but I'm trying my best.

(FR) Well, Father this is really beautiful. Thank you for witnessing God's work. My favorite answer to this, of course, is always the verse the psalmist wrote thousands of years ago, "Not to us O Lord, but to Your Name be the glory." He's the One, Jesus is the One, so we just have to give Him all the glory.

(FB) I really believe that, Father. You have to be honored for saying "yes" to what He wishes you to do.

(FR) It's a pleasure. I hope to be with you more, Father.

(FB) Oh, praise God! Let's hope so.

(FR) I think you are a chosen one.

(M) Yes, and I would like to say that I believe both of you are truly "chosen ones" to Mary's Helpers. I received confirmation from the two of you, on the same day, that you would write for our newsletter. That's great. I have to give Mary's Helpers a little plug, because we're going to have some interesting stories in our newsletter. We're looking forward to it. Praise God! Thank you, Father, for calling us. I appreciate it very, very much, and I'm sure our listeners do, too.

(FB) You are more than welcome. God bless both of you.

The following are highlights from the radio program taped on July 9, 1989.

(F) Good morning to you, Margaret, and to all the listeners out there. It is good to be back with you, and I feel very honored to be on this program.

(M) We are the honored ones, Father. I would like you to give us a reflection on Our Lady's message of Medjugorje of June 25, 1989. Because we have been hearing such wonderful words from Her, we need to listen and live the messages. I'm sure you will give us a beautiful reflection.

(F) Come, Holy Spirit, fill our hearts with Your burning love, and enlighten our minds.

(M) The message for the Eighth Anniversary, June 25, 1989:

"Dear Children, Today I call you to live my messages which I have been giving you for the past eight years. This is a time of grace, and I desire that the grace of God be great for every single one of you. I am blessing you, and I love you with a special kind of love. Thank you for responding to my call."

(F) Mary calls us to live the messages she has been giving us for the past eight years. What are these messages? Are they urgent messages to reform our lives? These messages are basic messages of the Gospel. Jesus gave us His holy Mother to remind us to reform our lives and turn back to God. That's what conversion means. We turn from evil and turn toward good. We must go from the negative to the positive in order to make our lives worthwhile instead of empty ones. We can do this through prayer, particularly the Rosary. Mary asks us to pray the fifteen mysteries of the Rosary every day. As a Servite, I also pray the Seven Sorrows Rosary which reminds us of the principle sorrows of Our Blessed Mother's life, the Mother of Sorrows. Mary wants us to pray the fifteen mysteries every day, go to daily Mass, if possible, and to confess our sins monthly.

Many people go to psychologists or psychiatrists to work out their problems. Very often, a good confession can do more good than long sessions on a doctor's couch, and it doesn't cost anything. We don't like to hear the word penance, because it sounds like a rough way to go. The discipline that comes from penance is beautifying. Mary asks us to fast on Friday as well as another day of the week. She recommends Wednesday as the other fasting day. Friday and Wednesday are the traditional days of fasting. Friday is important because Mary wants us to remember the Passion of Her Son, as well as Her compassion under the Cross. Prayer, penance, fasting, conversion, monthly confession, daily Mass, and the fifteen mysteries of the Rosary daily doesn't sound like too much, does it? If we live these messages, we will receive many graces. Mary has asked for a "Year of the Youth" of the world, and She directs her words to them. Of course, this includes all of us who are young at heart. She gives each one of us a special blessing, and a special touch of Her love while thanking us for responding to Her call. Amen.

(M) Father, I know you are scheduled to leave for Medjugorje next week. Could you tell us about some of the healings that have occurred at your healing services?

(F) Yes, Margaret, I am leaving a week from today with an Irish pilgrimage out of Belfast. One healing that comes to mind is that of a man who suffered from Parkinson's disease. He came to the cemetery behind the church, and was healed instantly. A forty year old lady who was born a deaf mute was healed. The first thing she heard with any clarity was a donkey braying on the top of the mountain where the Cross is located. The wonderful thing about this story is the donkey could not be found. It was hidden in the bushes, but she found him. Upon finding him, she gave him a big hug. These are just two of the many healings that occur in Medjugorje.

The following are highlights taken from the radio program on December 17, 1989.

(F) It is always a great joy to speak about Our Blessed Lady. I am a Servant of Mary, and I enjoy speaking about her, especially her messages from Medjugorje.

(M) We are going to go right into the message, and then Father will give the meditation on the message of November 25, 1989.

"Dear Children, I am inviting you, for years, by these messages which I am giving you. Little Children, by means of the messages, I wish to make a very beautiful mosaic in your hearts, so I might be able to present each

one of you to God like the original image. Therefore, little children, I desire that your decision be free before God, because He has given you your freedom. Therefore, pray so that, free from any influence of satan, you may decide only for God. I am praying for you before God, and I am seeking your surrender to God. Thank you for having responded to my call."

(F) Our Lady, thank you for this message, and we hope we can carry it out. In this message, we have to recall the Sixth Station of the Cross where Veronica wipes the face of Jesus. In the Sixth Station, Veronica, whose name means "true image," gave her veil to Jesus to wipe His Holy Face, and He left His image on her veil. God created a perfect image when He created Adam and Eve. A mosaic is significant, because it is a work of art which is made up of different colored tiny stones that make a piece of art. That's what Our Blessed Lady would like to happen to all of us. She wants us to become the original image of ourselves as little children. As Jesus said, "A little child shall lead them." We must become like little children again, and restore the image that God first created when He made us. Thank You, Jesus, and thank you, Mary. We want to be restored to Your original image. Amen.

I would, also, like to share with you a beautiful story about a man by the name of Bernard Ellis. Mr. Ellis, who is Jewish, received a great healing through Our Lady of Medjugorje. In 1980, when I was in Belfast, a lady asked me to pray with her. She was standing in for a certain Bernard Ellis and his family. Bernard heads up a large stainless steel corporation. At the time we were praying, he was in Malaysia. As we prayed, believe it or

39

not, he was delivered from a very, very deep depression that he had for a long time. On his return trip to England, he began instructions and became Catholic. Since then we have become very good friends. As a result of this healing, Mr. Ellis is erecting a building, in Medjugorje, for handicapped children who are not financially able to make the trip to Medjugorje.

This morning, I want to include in my interview something about Mary's Helpers. The Holy Father has encouraged groups such as Mary's Helpers in his "Apostolic Exhortation on the Laity." You have to bow to the evidence that says these communities, like Mary's Helpers, are an idea of who's time has come. Of course, Vatican II strongly encourages acts of participation of the laity in the various aspects of Church life. One of the great joys I had on this trip, was a side trip to Rome where I was able to have an audience with the Holy Father. These direct words with the Holy Father were due to our new Prior General, Father Moons. It was thrilling as always, and I thank him.

BEGINNING OF HEALING MINISTRY

The following are highlights taken from the radio program on September 23, 1990.

(M) Father, I would like you to tell us how you started with your healing ministry.

(F) I'm in a religious order called the Servants of Mary, and we wanted to start a foundation of our Order in Ireland. Father James Mary Keane wanted to found the Order in Ireland due to the number of Servites already established there. We started in Benburb, County Tyrone which is in Northern Ireland. From the beginning, people would come to be blessed, and some would return to say that they were cured of their illnesses. Before we knew it, bus loads of people were coming to be blessed. To this day, I still receive letters from people in Ireland telling me of their healing.

(M) Father, do you remember the Deacon who came to be blessed by you when we had our pilgrimage to Sterrett, Alabama?

(F) Yes, it was the Feast of the Assumption, August 15, 1989. I cannot recall his name, but they brought him in a special van equipped with oxygen. He was very weak, and not expected to live due to cancer. He had lost his voice, which is a severe blow for a Deacon who cannot preach the Gospel. For those who do not know, Sterrett is the place where Marija Pablovich, one of the six visionaries from Medjugorje, lived for several months when she donated one of her kidneys to her brother,

Andre. While she was there, she received visitations from Our Lady.

(M) The same Deacon came back for the Feast of the Assumption in 1990. Tell them about that father.

(F) The Deacon got up after the Communion of the Mass, and told us about his healing. He told us his cancer was in complete remission. He had regained his strength, his voice returned, and he was walking around like you and me. We all gave praise to the Lord with him.

(M) Father has just returned from Medjugorje. Tell us what happened on this particular pilgrimage.

(F) On the Hill of Apparitions, we had some beautiful manifestations of Our Lady's visit. One night, before Our Lady's arrival, lightning, like lights, came through the crowd, and a star moved toward the mountain to the Cross. The stronger we sang "Ave, Ave," the stronger the light from the star brightened. Finally, it disappeared. It was one of the most beautiful happenings I've experienced. When I am in Medjugorje, it is a tradition to hold a healing service. A beautiful German lady, Catherine Padanosky, witnessed that she was completely healed of cancer after she came to our healing service in May, 1990. When she returned home, a neighbor asked her to bring her fourteen year old blind son to Medjugorje. In June, 1990, we prayed over him, and anointed his eyes. I asked him to open his eyes, and he said in German, "I can see." He was asked to look at some print, and he could see the writing. Everyone was rejoicing about this as a special touch from Our Lady on Her anniversary. Praise God!

(M) Father, tell us about the Shrine of Our Lady of Walsenham in England.

(F) This is a National Shrine of Our Lady which dates back to the Middle Ages. Both kings and paupers made pilgrimages to the shrine. In fact, King Henry VIII went there before he broke away from Rome. In three different dreams, Michelleis was shown the Holy House of Nazareth, the home of the Holy Family. Through her dreams, she was instructed to erect another one to the dimensions of the original. As the Chronicle said, "The widow was full of glad." Michelleis began to wonder where the chapel should be placed. Going out to the meadow early one morning, she found two places where neither moisture nor dew was found. In her eagerness, she did not consult Our Lady. She chose the nearest site, and the strangest thing happened. The carpenters dug the foundation to her measurements, but, when they came to erect the little chapel, no piece would agree with the geometry as stated by the Chronicle in Old English. In great distress, they laid down their tools and went home as the widow had commanded them. During her nightly prayers, Our Lady told her to locate the chapel two hundred feet from the first place. When the carpenters returned the next day to wrestle with the problem, they found the chapel completed. It was built two hundred feet from the original foundation on the second piece of dry ground furthest from the twin well.

REFLECTIONS ON THE BOOK THE POEM OF THE MAN GOD

The following is a transcript of the radio program taped on September 13, 1992 between Margaret Trosclair and Father Rookey.

(M) Today, we have a special guest with us. Many of you have heard me talk about him so often that I know he is not a stranger to many of you. It is indeed a pleasure to have Father Peter Mary Rookey, the Healing Priest, here today. He has traveled all over the world, and he is renown for his healing ministry. The Lord works very powerfully through him, and many of you, who have attended his services, know the Lord is with him. It is my pleasure to introduce Father Peter Mary Rookey. It is good to have you here today, Father.

(F) It is a great honor to be with you, Margaret, the Foundress of Mary's Helpers who is doing such great work for Our Blessed Lady.

(M) Thank you, Father. We want to hear more about you, because, in this time of our lives, it seems we need God so desperately. We are searching, and many of us don't really know just how to open our hearts for Jesus to come into it. Maybe you could help us with that.

(F) I would like to say what immediately came to my mind when you said you wanted to hear about me. I must, as John the Baptist said, decrease and Jesus must increase. I am, as my name says, just a "Rookie" in His service as a Servant of Mary. I come to you today to upstage Jesus and Our Blessed Mother, whom God upstaged more than

44

we will ever be able to in honoring Her as the Mother of Jesus.

(M) Father, many listeners of this program have told me that they pray, but that they feel God is not listening to them. Could you say something on this?

(F) I believe my answer is from the Lord. We are all involved in praying for favors, and God wants us to ask Him for everything, even tiny things. However, sometimes we feel God is not answering our prayers, and that, of course, is an insult to God. God always answers our prayers. Naturally, we want to see results from our prayers, but actually our praying for something is making us into the image of God. We have to establish a relationship. God is God, and I am His creature. I am depending on Him, and I am being enriched, simply, by praying. I often think of Saint Monica. She would not be a saint today if it wouldn't have been for her wayward son, for whom she prayed for thirty-three years. If Augustine, her son, had not been the evil person he was until he converted to the Lord, she probably would not be Saint Monica. By prayer, she was formed into the image of Christ, and became a more perfect Christian. We never lose when we pray. I would like to quote from Mother Theresa of Calcutta. "God did not call us to be successful, but to be faithful." In other words, to quote our Lord, "He who perseveres to the end, he will be saved." This persevering praying is what makes us great and holy. It is nice to see results of prayers, but it is not necessary. We never lose by praying for our healing, or whatever we feel we need in our lives.

(M) Thank you, Father. I understand exactly what you're saying, because so many of us are praying for someone,

Our Lady of Sorrows

perhaps a family member, children, or whatever, but the fact is that prayers put our lives together. Father, from all your travels around the world, could you tell us about the miracles that have happened, also, many people are interested in the book, **The Poem of the Man God**. Could we discuss this?

(F) Yes, thank you, Margaret. I would like to mention that many, many miracles happened in England during the time I spent there in May of this year, 1992. The Daily Sport, a tabloid out of London, had a large write up about a young man who had Aids. He came to us while we were at the Holy Ghost Church in Balaam which is a suburb of London. Last year, in April, 1991, I told him, that in order for him to be healed, he had to make an agreement with the Lord not to follow this type of life style anymore. He did so on the spot. He prayed the **Miracle Prayer**, and 'rested in the Spirit' after we prayed over him. When he got up, he claimed his healing immediately because he felt so wonderful. This year, when we returned to England, his doctors gave him a clean bill of health. This young man, whose father was a member of the House of Lords, the upper house of the English government, along with his doctors came out publicly about his healing. The headline said, "Aids, Hell of a Top Lord." You know, he was embarrassed by all this publicity, but now, he is rejoicing that his son has been healed. However, this is only one of the many, many healings that hit the press.

(M) Father has been with us since September 7th at the start of the Novena of Our Lady of Sorrows, and so many beautiful things have happened. I wish I could share them with you, but we want to hear a little about **The Poem of the Man God**. So many people are concerned about reading this book, because they have heard, as well as read, that this book should not be read. Would you tell us more about this?

(F) Yes, Margaret. I don't know if you would call Cindy Cain a visionary, but she seems to receive messages from Our Lady. On March 23, 1992, she received a message which reads as follows. "My precious little ones, I thank you all for your prayers and sacrifices given to my Son through my Immaculate Heart. Your faith and obedience cause all Heaven to rejoice. Little ones, your Heavenly Mother, by God's authority, knows how insidiously the evil one works, and he has sown the seed of darkness and clouds of confusion upon my little children. He, the father of half truths, has seduced so many of my children, and is leading you away from my Son, from the Truth, by his clever attack upon **The Poem of the Man God,** which is the work of a Secular Servite by the name of Maria Valtorta. Yes, my children, to my chosen one, my choice in Medjugorje, I have confirmed the supernatural origin of this most valuable work, **The Poem of the Man God**. I have said it may be read, it should be read, because my Son desired for all His little ones to come to an intimate relationship with Him. There are many angry voices, which deride anything found as spiritual nourishment in this work, who are being deceived, and do not clearly see the purity of this work. I ask then of each of you to pray to the Almighty God that He may cause the confusion regarding this work to abate. Yet, I solemnly tell you there will be yet many angry words, accusations hurled against this blessed work given to the world by my Divine Son, **The Poem of the Man God**, and all who defend the Truth. Do not be deceived, pray hard, and pray to the Holy Spirit for true discernment." I am bringing this up, because in the introduction of this terrific work, it tells how Pope Pius XII instructed my brother Servite priests, Father Bert Ciachin, and Father Migliorini, to publish it as it is. Father Ciachin is still living, and he is a living witness to all that the Pope told the three of them.

(M) You're saying its okay to read **The Poem of the Man God**. I think many were under the impression that this book was to take the place of the Bible. Father, can you tell us about this?

(F) That's an accusation, and its completely without foundation. In fact, we perceive the Sacred Scriptures with renewed faith and open hearts when reading this terrific account of the life of Our Lord. Of course, the life of Mary figures very prominently in it. I would say that it is difficult to believe these accusations when we have people, like Pope Pius XII, who perused the book before he told the three Servite priests to publish it. Pope Paul VI sent a beautiful letter to our Father Roschini, who is the head of the Marianum which is the Servite University in Rome, as to his preference of this book. However, it seems that there were many who were against this book. According to Cardinal Ratzinger, one of the great stumbling blocks is the fact that **The Poem of the Man God** was put on the index of forbidden books. There was another great book, about Our Lady, **The Mystical City of God.** It was put on the index twice. I'm glad to say that a great Secular Servite, Pope Innocent XI, went over the heads of those who put it on the index, and stated that these books could be read with impunity, by all. There is no known prohibition against reading **The Poem of the Man God** or **The Mystical City of God** at this date.

(M) Well, Father, I wish we could go on, because it is so interesting to hear you talk about this book. Because of the lack of time, Father will not be able to pray the **Miracle Prayer**. I invite you to listen to radio station WTIX 690 AM on your dial at 9:00 A.M. immediately following this program. Father will then pray the **Miracle Prayer**. Father, I want to thank you for being here today, as our special guest.

(F) Thank you, Margaret Trosclair, and God bless us all.

The following are highlights from the radio program broadcast live on September 12, 1993.

(M) Father, you were in Medjugorje for the Twelfth Anniversary on June 25, 1993. Is there any special healing that occurred at that time?

(F) I have spoken to you many times about the way the Lord is going about the earth "laying hands" on people and healing them. The blind see, and the deaf mutes hear as well as speak for the first time. At our prompting, their first words are "Jesus and Mary." People come to the services in wheelchairs, but they leave the services pushing their wheelchairs. There's a healing explosion going on throughout the world. Our Lord is making His presence felt strongly in order for us to increase our faith. He said, "If you don't believe My Words, believe My works." A twenty-eight year old Romanian dentist, who was obviously possessed, came to our healing service in Medjugorje. He was unable to eat, and when he did, he had terrible pain and diarrhea. Twice he tried fasting for long periods of time, but to no avail. He was unable to rid himself of this evil spirit. What the devil put him through is unbelievable. He would lie on the floor with one leg up. The other leg would fly up while his hands would flap strongly on the floor. From a prone position, the demon would have him standing on his head. When he started hissing like a snake, I told the devil, "You've been hissing like a snake, I command you to go into a snake." At that moment, a priest who was looking at the proceedings saw a dark form exit from the tent and go into the ground. The young man was delivered that day. He stood before the assembly, and gave his wonderful testimony. Finally, he was able to eat, but, more importantly, he was free and at peace. Another wonderful healing happened to a lady by the name of Bernadette who was from Ireland. She and her husband were married for six years, but they had no children. Wanting children desperately, they came to us to be blessed. Bernadette recently called us to announce that she is eight months pregnant with twins, and the mother is 47 years young. Praise God!

The following testimonies are taken from the healing service at Our Lady of Sorrows Novena in September, 1992.

I felt drawn to attend the nine day novena to Our Mother of Sorrows at Immaculate Conception Church in Marrero, Louisiana. Up until a few years ago, I wasn't aware there was such a novena to Our Lady. I would attend Mass on Her feast days, but nothing more.

I looked forward to hearing the priests talk on each of Our Lady's sorrows, and my heart was deeply touched. It made me realize how much Mary suffered, with most of it being silent suffering. We were invited to stay for Father Rookey's healing service. He is such a powerful instrument of Our Lord. God uses him in the healing ministry, but he also gave him a sense of humor. He is such a special priest, and we love him very much.

All through the novena, something was happening to me which is very hard to describe. I experienced some of Our Lady's pain. Every time I would look at her statue or the banner on the podium, I would feel a great sadness, and tears would well up in my eyes. I've always loved our Mother Mary. In this novena, she showed me how she shared all of Her Son's pain.

On the night of Father Rookey's healing service, I was leading the Rosary with some ladies from Mary's Helpers when, all of a sudden, I felt this force pushing me off the kneeler. At that time Father Rookey was praying over two men. I decided that instead of praying for myself for a healing, I would pray for my friend, Anita, who was about to have open heart surgery. Father Rookey told us that in praying for others needs, we truly are receiving many blessings from God.

For a number of years, I suffered with a lot of pain in my right shoulder and elbow. I would experience some relief when I would get a cortisone shot, but the pain always came back. All during the novena it hurt. I knew I wanted to help carry the statue of Our Lady during the procession. I signed up, but, with so many others wanting to help, I thought there was little chance I would get to help carry the statue. Finally, someone asked me, and I took her place. I never left that spot until we returned to Church. The whole time we walked my shoulder hurt, but I kept offering all my pain to Jesus and Mary. My spiritual son, Gregory, continued asking if he could help me in any way, but I kept refusing. Because I had been ill for three weeks prior to the event, I thanked God for giving me the strength to attend. About three or four days after the novena, I suddenly realized I no longer had the pain in my shoulder or elbow. Praise the Lord!

It is now one year later, and still no pain. I realized I should have written this sooner, but, like many others, I wanted to see if it was really from God. Thank You, Jesus, for all of the blessings I received at the 1992 and 1993 novenas.

Grace Winn

When I attended the novena to Our Lady of Sorrows in September of 1992, I had no idea how my life would forever change through Fr. Rookey's ministry. This was all part of God's plan through His mother Mary as she continued to lead me closer to Her Son, Jesus. She had called me back to confession after an almost sixteen year absence.

During this solemn nine day novena, I felt as if Mary was guiding me through a total spiritual purging. Each night I prayed, cried and searched my soul. For the very first time in my life, I realized that Jesus was not the sole Victim of my sins. I crucified God, the Father, and Mary, His Mother, too! I also realized that my life did not belong to me, but to God!

As I sat in the rear of the church witnessing my first healing service being conducted by Father Rookey, I watched the faces of those "resting in the Spirit." I knew not what they were experiencing, but I HOPED for just a little bit of it. Finally, I stood to the right of the altar gazing at the Blessed Sacrament in Exposition. I felt in awe of God, and at the same time, blessed to be so close to His physical Presence. Then Fr. Rookey stood before me. It seemed, like he had hardly touched my forehead when a total relaxation enveloped my body, and I was lowered to the floor. I was resting in Jesus' Holy Spirit! A beautiful smiling Christ stood before me with outstretched arms. In my mind I understood Him to say "Come to Me My child." Oh, how I tried to move my body up from the floor to go to Jesus. There I stayed as if glued in place. It is very difficult to humanly describe what I next experienced. Although I could feel my physical body on that floor, it was as if I were lifted up out of my body to Jesus. Jesus held me in His arms, and hugged me in the most comforting, tender and loving embrace. His all encompassing love, and His mercy seemed to flood my soul in ecstasy until I felt it might burst from sheer joy! I know Jesus healed me spiritually through Fr. Rookey that night.

NEVER would I have thought my "yes" to Jesus would lead to an association with Mary's Helpers who sponsored that novena. NEVER would I have thought Mary would lead me to Medjugorje in June 1994 with Fr. Rookey. NEVER would I have thought there would be the first Secular Order of the Servants of Mary in the South as a direct result of Fr. Rookey's intervention. NEVER would I have thought I would be part of that, and become a true Servant of Mary myself.

I HOPED to receive just a little bit of the Holy Spirit through Fr. Rookey. God chose to grant me more than I could ever begin to share in a few words. As I sat atop Apparition Hill in Medjugorje, I PRAYED God might not find me selfish in requesting just a little bit of Fr. Rookey's holiness to rub off on me. Oh! to be so richly blessed.

Lenora Martinez, S.O.S.M.

53

Father Peter Mary Rookey, O.S.M.

FATHER'S LOVE FOR THE ROSARY

The following are highlights from the radio program recorded on August 14, 1994.

(M) Father, tomorrow is the Feast of the Assumption. Would you tell us about the Assumption?

(F) Our Lady had the honor and privilege of being taken into heaven in a complete state. When a mortal dies, the body remains on earth and turns to dust. We are reminded of this on Ash Wednesday when the priests put ashes and say to us, "Remember, you are dust and unto dust you shall return." Mary, because of Her sinlessness, was brought, body and soul, to heaven, immediately upon her passing. Mary went to heaven in somewhat the same way as Jesus went back to Heaven in the Ascension. I had the great privilege of being in St. Peter's Square in Rome on August 15, 1954, when Pope Pius XII officially declared the dogma that Mary was brought up body and soul into heaven. By definition, a dogma is a principal believed to be true. The Assumption is part of our faith. It was always believed by the Church, but it hadn't previously been given the honor of being declared by the Church as a truth that was to be accepted and believed. There is no direct reference to the Assumption in the Bible even though it has always been believed by the Church. John says at the end of the Gospel, "There are many other things Jesus taught and said. If they were all written, the world could not contain all the books that would have to be written." Therefore, we have to accept what Jesus gave through Peter. "You are Peter and upon this rock I will build My Church." We have to accept what has always been believed, and that is why the Pope was able to declare the Assumption as dogma. Interestingly, the privilege of the Assumption goes hand in hand with another privilege, but from a different Pope. In 1854, it was declared that Mary, from the first moment of Her conception in the womb of Her mother, was kept from all stain of sin. I don't find this difficult to understand. Once God decided that Jesus, the Son of God, was to come to us through the womb of a woman, we knew that this woman would have to be devoid of all sin. God and sin cannot be together. It is like saying yes and no at the same time which is a complete contradiction. It is not difficult to understand that God preserved Mary from all sin in the womb of Her mother, Saint Ann. The Immaculate Conception was pronounced as a dogma by Pope Pius IX in 1854. Four years later, 1858, Mary appeared to Bernadette Soubirous, an uneducated peasant girl in Lourdes, France. Mary told Bernadette she was the Immaculate Conception. These two events mark the beginning of Mary's existence. I've been asked by people about many of the Church's teachings that are not in the Bible. As stated previously, there is nothing mentioned in the Bible about the Assumption or the Immaculate Conception. You will find these teachings backed up by Scripture in the constant belief of the Church. Because of this, many Christians find it hard to believe since it is not in the Bible.

The earliest writings that we have in the New Testament come from 60 A.D. Jesus died in 33 A.D., and, I believe, the earliest writings came from the Epistle of Saint Paul to the Thessalonians. The Thessalonians were Christians who had no New Testament. They only had the prophets, Moses, and the Old Testament. Before Jesus left us, according to Mark's account, He told His apostles, "Go into the whole world and preach the Gospel to all nations. Baptize them in the Name of the Father, the Son and the Holy Spirit. Teach them to observe what I have told you." Jesus told this to His apostles before He went back to the right hand of His Father, which is called the Ascension. He completed the Old Testament. It is the Church that Jesus gave us that must tell us what the Scripture means.

(M) Father, there are so many of us in the world who are unforgiving. Many of us would like to be healed, but we carry a lot of hurt within us. Would you like to touch on this subject?

(F) I can give you a practical example of exactly what you are talking about to our listeners. When we were in England in May, 1992, we were asked to pray over a young man who had six days to live. He had bone marrow cancer. As we began to pray over him in his hospital bed, the Lord directed me to ask him a question. I asked the young man, "Is there anyone in your life you must forgive?" He nodded and said, "Yes, Father." We began to pray that this unforgivness would be healed. His tears began to flow, and he wept profusely. The crying this young man experienced was an outward sign of the inner healing that was taking place. We then invoked the powerful intercession of our Blessed Mother, and my brother Servite, Saint Peregrine, the Cancer Saint. The lady, who requested the prayers for this young man, attended one of our healing services a year later. She witnessed that the young man had recently returned from Australia. He told his friend, that at the moment he forgave that person in his life, he was healed. The young man is now working on a crocodile farm in Australia.

The following are highlights *from the radio program on October 2, 1994.*

(M) Father, as you know, on October 7, we will be celebrating the Feast of Our Lady of the Rosary. Today, I would like for you to talk about the Rosary.

(F) The Rosary comes from the Latin word Rosa, and a rosarium would be a wreath of roses. Therefore, we have the word Rosary. The wreath of roses is made up of the greatest prayers ever given us. It was given to us by the Son of God, Jesus, Who was approached by the Apostles who asked Him to teach them how to pray. Jesus said, "When you pray, pray like this:

Our Father, Who art in Heaven,
hallowed be Thy Name, Thy kingdom come,
Thy Will be done on earth as It is in Heaven.
Give us this day our daily bread,
and forgive our trespasses as we forgive
those who trespass against us, and lead us not into
temptation, but deliver us from evil. Amen."

Some versions of the prayer add, "For Thine is the Kingdom and the Power and the Glory for ever and ever. Amen." The Rosary is made up of **the Our Father**, and the words of the Angel Gabriel who went to Mary asking Her to be the Mother of God. In Luke 2, we find the Angel Gabriel being sent by God to a town in Galilee, Nazareth, to a virgin espoused to a man by the name of Joseph. The virgin's name is Mary. Upon entering,

Gabriel greeted her with these words, "Hail Mary, full of grace, the Lord is with you. Blessed are you among women!" What a compliment! When Mary went to visit her cousin, Elizabeth, who, at her advanced age, was six months pregnant with John the Baptist, cried out "Blessed are you among women, and Blessed is the Fruit of your womb." Elizabeth, who was filled with the Holy Spirit, was given to understand that Mary had conceived the Savior. Those are the words that are prayed mostly in the Rosary. In the beginning of the Rosary, we renew our basic belief in God by praying **the Apostles' Creed.**

"I believe in God, the Father Almighty,
Creator of heaven and earth, and in Jesus Christ,
His only Son, Our Lord, Who was conceived
by the Holy Spirit, born of the virgin Mary,
suffered under Pontius Pilate, was crucified,
died, and was buried. He descended into hell,
and on the third day, He rose again from the dead,
He ascended into Heaven and sits at the
right hand of the Father Almighty, from thence
He shall come to judge the living and the dead.
I believe in the Holy Spirit, the Holy Catholic
Church, the Communion of Saints, the
forgiveness of sins, the Resurrection of the
body, and the life in the world to come. Amen."

After praying **the Lord's Prayer** or **the Our Father** as it is most often called, and **the Hail Mary** ten times, we close the meditation on the particular mystery with the doxology, a short hymn, of praise to the Father, the Son, and the Holy Spirit.

"Glory be to the Father, the Son,
and the Holy Spirit as it was in the
beginning, is now, and ever shall be,
world without end. Amen."

Start the Rosary by making the **Sign of the Cross**, and say **the Apostles' Creed** on the Crucifix. On the first large bead say **the Our Father** which is followed by three **Hail Marys** on the three smaller beads. Before the last large bead say the **Glory Be to the Father**, and then on the large bead announce the First Mystery followed by **the Our Father**. Now, say ten **Hail Marys** while meditating on the Mystery. Say the **Glory Be to the Father**. After each decade say the following prayer requested by Our Lady at Fatima. "O my Jesus, forgive us our sins, save us from the fires of hell, lead all souls to Heaven, especially those who have most need of Your Mercy." Announce the Second Mystery, and say one **Our Father**, ten **Hail Marys**, one **Glory be to the Father**, and the requested prayer. Repeat this with the Third, Fourth, and Fifth Mysteries in the same manner. After the five decades are completed, say the **Hail, Holy Queen**. Generally the Joyful Mysteries are said on Monday and Thursday. The Sorrowful Mysteries are said on Tuesday and Friday with the Glorious ones being said on Wednesday and Saturday. Each of the mysteries are recommended for Sunday. The Rosary is made up of mental prayer which is a form of meditating on the mysteries of our faith, and vocal prayers. We use vocal prayers when we say **the Lord's Prayer** and the **Hail Mary**; however, the Lord and our Blessed Mother keep reminding us that our prayers must come from our heart. Vocal prayer must come from the meditation and the mind. If it doesn't, it simply becomes words without feeling.

(M) Father, many people have said that praying the Rosary is repetitious. What can you tell these people who feel this way?

(F) The Rosary should not be prayed rapidly. It is not coming from the heart if it lacks meditation. Our Lady, in Her many apparitions in Medjugorje, keeps reminding us to pray from the heart. The Psalmists, the Prophets, and Jesus remind us many times to pray from the heart. Jesus said, "These people honor Me with their lips, but their heart is far from Me." Do we ever tire of hearing "I love you" from our spouse or from friends. We should think of the Rosary as saying over and over to Our Lord and to His Blessed Mother, "I love You." It would never be considered repetitious by them. Just as we like to hear these words, they like to hear them from their children. In October, 1993, a Methodist minister, Roger King, whom I had never met, phoned me one day out of the blue. He told me someone had given him a Rosary when he was seriously ill. At that time, he began to pray the Rosary. Minister King became well, and, to this day, is still saying the Rosary.

Seven Holy Founders

Seven Holy Founders and Servite Saints

(M) We have Father Peter Mary Rookey from Chicago with us today. He is a Servite priest who is also known as "the Healing Priest." It is good to have you with us today, Father.

(F) Thank you so much for inviting me to speak on a subject that is very dear to both of us. Margaret is not only the Foundress of Mary's Helpers, but she is also a Secular Servite. Margaret, we will start with the Seven Holy Founders of the Servite Order. Actually, Our Lady was the one who began the Servants of Mary. These seven saints dedicated their Order entirely to Our Blessed Mother, especially to the Mother of Sorrows.

(M) Father, I did not realize that Our Lady of Sorrows was so dear to me until I met you almost eight years ago. I am sure you brought this devotion out in me. I had been wearing Her medal since 1984 which was two years before I met you. The Lord knows what is for us. I am sure you have much to tell us about the Founders of the Servites.

(F) All of the Popes, especially Pope John Paul II, have always told religious orders to return to their roots. By speaking about the Seven Holy Founders, I am answering his request, and at the same time, renewing the spirit of the Servite Order. We must renew ourselves by constantly meditating on Our Blessed Lord and His life which are the mysteries of our faith.

(M) Weren't the Seven Holy Founders merchants?

(F)   Yes, they were wool merchants who had prospered. They lived in Florence, Italy, in the early Thirteenth Century when it was a great commercial center. At this time in history, it was a significant political power, as well as a center for spiritual renewal. In order to understand the background of the Servite Order, we have to go back in time to the Franciscans, Dominicans and Carmelites which were known as mendicant religious orders. The mendicants were named from the word mendicare which means "to beg" in Latin. These poor friars had no personal possessions, and they begged for alms. The mendicants, which were founded on poverty, can be contrasted to the monastic orders which built large facilities incorporating farms around their monasteries. Saint Benedict, the founder of the monastic system in the western world, made his monks take a vow of stability. They learned to be self supportive, and, in turn, taught the people around them. The monks, also, looked after the people in their locale spiritually. During the Thirteenth Century, towns, and cities began to develop. The friars went all over preaching the Gospel which created a new approach to the faith. The monks sanctified people in their own areas, but the friars went out to preach in various towns and the country side.

The Seven Holy Founders began as the Friar Servants of Mary who belonged to a sodality called the Praisers of Our Lady. A sodality is a devotional or charitable society in the Roman Catholic Church. It was after one of the meetings of the sodality that Our Lady appeared to each one of them individually inviting them to come together and to give themselves to prayer, fasting and penance. Records show that some of these seven wool merchants were married while others were single or widowed. It is believed that these seven shared the same interests in the penitential and Marian movements. Through these interest, they built up strong ties of friendship with each other. The Seven also wanted to break their ties with the material world, and to live together in a community setting which would enable them to support one another in every way. Before starting their community life, they provided for their families, and gave the rest of their wealth to the Church as well as to the poor. The Seven Holy Founders kept nothing in the material sense for themselves. It was important to these Seven to take time and think about the important things in life.

(M) What happened after the Seven decided to come together as a community?

(F) Everyone must understand that the Servites developed during a time of upheaval and change in the world, as well as in the Church. No longer were people staying in the country to farm. Trade was growing and exploration of the world was beginning. Education was changing which caused new ways of thinking. With the growth of these cities came new problems such as crime, corruption, poverty, materialism, urban gangs, and urban violence. War on a larger scale became very viable because of the growing prosperity. At this time, there was a great political struggle going on between the Holy Roman Emperor and the Holy Father.

The Church of the Thirteenth Century realized it had to change in order to catch up with the changing time. Because the Church had centered itself around farming villages and monastery schools, it realized it had to change in order to keep up with the new life styles of the world. Many men and women turned to God with prayer and penance to combat the evil of the day that was growing. They refused to take part in any money making scheme hoping they could turn people to the ways of God.

The civil war that went on between the Holy Roman Emperor and the Holy Father was a fierce struggle. In fact, before the Seven founded their community, the strife found them split down the middle in their allegiance. However, when it was over. the Seven friends were able to forgive and forget. They loved each other so much they found it difficult to live away from each other for any length of time. I often tell people in the healing ministry that the One who has the worst case of Alzheimer's in the world is the Heavenly Father, because He not only forgives, He forgets. Our Lady appeared to the Seven men in 1233, and by 1242 they were living a very intense community life. The Seven friars' foundation is based on laymen, the Servants of Mary, who had great devotion to Mary. They moved into a dwelling in Caffagio which is just outside the original walls of Florence. The Church of the Holy Annunciation stands in this location, and it was their first Church. The Holy Founders were under the guidance of Saint Peter of Verona. It was under his spiritual guidance that the Seven sought even more solitude. They had been caring for the sick and the needy, but they felt they needed more for their spiritual well being. Seeking greater solitude, the group, directed by Our Lady, moved up the mountain to Monte Senario, an isolated, tree covered area about twelve miles from Florence. While they were in the mountains, their relationship with Mary grew, and their devotion to Her grew stronger. They accepted, as their rule, the Rule of Saint Augustine which dates back to the Fourth Century. The rule of St. Augustine begins with these words, "Before all else, brothers, God is to be loved and then our neighbor." These words were certainly exemplified in their lives. After their time of retreat was over on Monte Senario, they were ready to come down from the mountain to actively start their ministry. The Seven Holy Founders established communities in Florence and Sienna. Over the next seven hundred years their communities were established and they were spreading the Word in every continent except Antarctica. As the Servite Order grew larger, the friars dedicated their churches to Mary and honored Her in their liturgical services. They especially honored the Feast of Our Lady of Sorrows. The Seven continued to witness to the importance of prayer and the importance of being unencumbered by the world. As you can see, not too much is known about the personal lives of the Seven Founders.

In a way, the details about their individual lives are not that important. The facts of their lives remain hidden somewhat like the life of Mary. Servites who have followed in the way of the Seven have preferred to honor them as a group because their holiness grew out of the love they shared as a community. In 1888, they were canonized together by Pope Leo XIII. This was the only time in history that the Church canonized the entire founding community of confessors. The Seven were also buried together in one tomb. They lived in love together in life, and they were not separated in death.

(M) The Crucifix that you use to bless people contains relics of all the Founders. Am I right?

Saint Peregrine

(F) Yes, it also contains relics of other Servite saints.

(M) Please give everyone in our listening audience a blessing.

(F) God's power is not limited by time or space. I bless you with the relics of the Seven Holy Founders. "Through the prayers and merits of Our Blessed Lady, the Seven Holy Founders, the Servants of Mary, and all the saints, may the blessing of Almighty God, the Father, the Son, and the Holy Spirit descend upon you, heal you and remain with you. Amen."

(M) Thank you, so much, Father for being here with us and telling us about these beautiful saints known as the Seven Holy Founders.

(F) It is a privilege and honor to be here with you, Margaret.

(M) We are going to do a series on six other Servite saints. Each week, we hope to give all of you information on the saints, because they are the ones Father always speaks about during his healing service. Father, I would like you to begin with Saint Peregrine.

(F) There are many more than six Servite saints, but I have chosen these special ones to talk about. Saint Peregrine is perhaps the best known of the Servite saints because of his healings of those who have suffered with cancer. As a youth in Italy, he was a member of a gang. Because of this, he has been invoked by recovering gang members, and youth who want to leave the life of a gang member. Gangs are a terrible scourge in society. Children who are resisting gang recruitment, families of gang members, communities suffering from the scourge of gangs, and victims of gang warfare have all turned to Saint Peregrine for his help. Many great saints did not start out as great individuals. In fact, many of them started out as vigorous enemies of the Church, and Saint Peregrine is no exception. He was born in 1265 in Forli, Italy. In those days, the Pope was not only the Chief Shepherd of the Church, but he was also the head of government for a large portion of central Italy. The Pope sent Saint Philip Benizi, another great Servite, to bring peace to the troubled republic of Forli. While addressing an angry mob in the town square, he urged the citizens to make peace with the Holy Father and return to the Sacraments.

Saint Philip was driven out of town by this gang. One of the most violent and outspoken leaders of this gang who drove him out of Forli was the eighteen year old Peregrine. He actually went up to Philip and struck him on the face. When Peregrine saw how Philip responded to the taunts and violence, he was truly touched. Philip responded to the mob by prayerfully interceding before God that they may be forgiven. Peregrine was ashamed of his behavior, as well as his aimless life. He realized that because of his hostile and violent behavior, he lacked peace of soul. Peregrine couldn't help but notice the peace that this Servant of Mary enjoyed. It became apparent to him that by giving of yourself, you gained much more than grabbing things for yourself.

Peregrine searched for some kind of direction for his life. His thoughts always turned to the Servants of Mary. He finally asked the Servites in Sienna if he could enter their Order, and he was accepted by them. Peregrine was assigned to his home town of Forli after his period of formation was over. He spent the remainder of his life in this location. As a Servite, he ministered to the sick and to the poor. During the Fourteenth Century, a number of famines plagued Italy, and Peregrine was a tireless advocate of the needs of the hungry. It has been said that several miraculous multiplications of food were attributed to his prayers for the starving. Peregrine had finally found his purpose as well as his goal in life. He found both in God.

Always conscious of his sinful past, Peregrine persued a strenuous penitential exercise. He would stand in prayer for long periods of time after he had put in many hours tending to the people of Forli. After many years, the constant standing took its toll on his legs. When he was sixty years of age, open sores developed on his right leg. A physician diagnosed these sores as cancerous, and ordered Peregrine's leg to be amputated. The night before the surgery, he dragged himself to the community room and prayed before the image of Christ on the Cross until he fell asleep. It seems the Lord came off the Cross, touched his wounds, and healed him instantly.

The word of his healing spread quickly. When he died twenty years later, at the age of eighty, he was already being venerated as a Saint. He is now the Patron Saint of all those who suffer from cancer, and also the Patron of his native city, as well as the Patron of Saint Rio Bronco Diocese in the Amazon region of Brazil. He was also declared, at one point, the Patron Saint of Spain.

Because Peregrine was such a wild man in his youth, it seems only right that he would be invoked to take care of another type of cancer, a cancer of society. Like physical cancer, gangs begin in one area and spread rapidly drawing in teens and primary school children. The scourge on humanity affects families already dealing with problems of poverty, below standard education, and poor housing. Initially, it seems that families are either ignorant of the fact that they have a family member involved in a gang, or they deny the family member is in a gang. Rather than seek professional help, the parents try to cover up for their children until its too late. Family units crumble and families deteriorate. People withdraw into the supposed security of their homes with violent crimes and drugs creating a pall of fear. The public streets, alleys, parks, and play grounds are given over to gang activity. Saint Peregrine overcame the physical disease as well as the spiritual disease through the grace of Jesus, Our Lord. Turning away from personal and social destruction to a constructive and spiritual life based on service, Saint Peregrine is a powerful example for the youth of today, their families, and urban neighborhoods in our nation as well as abroad.

(M) The Crucifix that Father Rookey uses for his blessings has a relic of Saint Peregrine in it.

(F) There have been many healings from cancer through the intercession of Saint Peregrine. In 1980, I was called to St. Luke Presbyterian Hospital in Chicago, to minister to a young Italian father about thirty years of age who was dying of bone marrow cancer. When I entered his room, I could not help notice his comatose state. I prayed and then blessed him with the relic of Saint Peregrine. I also blessed his wife. When I was getting ready to go, his wife asked me, "Father, would you mind putting the relic Crucifix in my husband's hand." She went on to say that when I placed the relic Crucifix in her hand, an electric shock went through her body. I agreed, and we placed the Crucifix with the relic of Saint Peregrine in his hand. The young man came out of the coma. When I assisted

St. Philip Benizi

at a Mass we had in his hospital room a few days later, he was sitting up and speaking clearly.

(M) Father, would you like to sum up with a little prayer?

(F) "Oh, great Saint Peregrine, you turned away from your gang companions and reformed your life, rejected violence, and reached out in service to your community. You were healed instantly from an incurable disease. Please intercede to God this healing of cancer, and stop the growth of gangs in our country. Thank you, Saint Peregrine. May the blessing of Almighty God, the Father, Son and Holy Spirit, through the prayers and merits of our Blessed Mother, Saint Peregrine and all our saints descend upon you, heal you and remain with you. Amen."

(M) Thank you, Father. I want to thank you once again for being here, and God bless you in all your work.

(F) It's a pleasure, Margaret. Thank you.

(M) Today, Father Peter Mary Rookey will talk about another Servite saint, Saint Philip Benizi. I know he will give us a beautiful understanding of this saint.

(F) You know, Margaret, every day I see great miracles from God through the intercession of the saints. We are nourished by the lives of the saints, and they have set such great examples for us. Throughout the centuries, the saints have always been invoked.

It is recorded that the Servite Order was founded in 1233, and 1233 is also the year Saint Philip was born in Florence, Italy. Philip was blessed from God with great intelligence and imagination. Because he came from a wealthy family, he was able to develop his natural abilities at the finest schools available. When he entered the Servites, he entered as a lay brother. For four years, his talents were not used to their fullest potential. You see, he thought himself very small compared to the greatness of God. He was invited to become a priest, and he rose very quickly through the ranks to become Prior General of the Servite Order. He, in fact, was so highly regarded by Rome that he was sent by the Holy Father on a peace mission to Forli. As you know, it was Philip who was attacked by the young Peregrine.

As Prior General, Philip was responsible for increasing the number of communities in the Order, as well as organizing them into provinces. Through all the wonderful and great things he did, he never once saw himself as anyone other than "Brother Philip." He held the office of Prior General practically to the day he died. His gifts were, so considerable and luminous that he was even considered to be Pope. When he completed his service as head of the Servites, he moved to Todi, the poorest house in the Servite Order. He died there in 1285, and is laid out under the altar in a glass urn. It is believed that Philip is responsible for giving the Order the title Servants of Mary. When he was just a little child, he saw the Seven men Mary had chosen to begin the Order. Upon seeing them, he said, "Behold the Servants of Mary." Philip also had a great devotion to our Blessed Lady. When he died, he was quickly proclaimed a saint by his contemporaries. This sainthood was not based on his brilliance or his diplomatic skills, but on his true concern for his brother

Servites. Philip truly loved his brothers. He was canonized in 1671.

I am going to give you two examples of how the Lord is still presenting Saint Philip to us. The first has to do with a Methodist Minister from the Green Bay area in Wisconsin, Reverend Roger King. Reverend King called the office in Chicago to ask what the Servite Order had to do with the Mother of Sorrows. He had been receiving locutions from someone who said she was the Mother of Sorrows. He was told he should pray to Saint Philip Benizi and Saint Peregrine. I was quite surprised at this. He knew nothing about these saints, but Our Lady wanted him to know they were very powerful. I told him something about them, and sent him some literature on our saints. Another beautiful tribute to Saint Philip has been occurring for over a year in our Basilica of Our Lady of Sorrows in Chicago. Above the main altar in the Basilica is a huge oil painting of St. Philip celebrating his first Mass. Angels were thought to have been heard and so the artist has angels above the altar. Our Lady has allegedly been appearing there every First Saturday for over a year, and I have seen her. Saint Philip is still very much with us.

(M) Father, thank you so much. Would you give a blessing for our folks out there?

(F) I will bless everyone with the relic of Saint Philip as God's power is not limited by time or space. "May almighty God bless you in the Name of the Father, Son and Holy Spirit through the prayers and merits of our Blessed Mother, Saint Philip Benizi, and all our saints and heal you and remain with you forever. Amen."

St. Juliana Mary Falconieri

(M) Thank you so much, Father Peter Mary Rookey.

(F) It is a pleasure, Margaret. Thank you.

(M) God bless you!

(M) Father Peter Mary Rookey will now tell us about another Servite Saint, Saint Juliana Mary Falconieri, O.S.M.

(F) Thank you, Margaret. It is always a great pleasure to speak about the Servite saints, especially Saint Juliana. Juliana, whose family name was Falconieri, was the Mother of the Servite sisters. She was born into a noble family in Florence, Italy at the end of the Thirteenth Century. When she was fifteen, she heard Saint Alexis, one of the Servite Founders, preach on divine judgment. It just so happened that Saint Alexis was also a Falconieri. While he preached, he impressed Juliana so much that she made a decision to turn away from her life of wealth and privilege. Juliana pursued her desire to learn more about the new Order of the Servants of Mary. Eventually, she asked the friars for admittance to the Order.

Juliana was joined by a number of other young women who also wanted to offer their life to Christ under the protection of Mary. This group of women gathered for daily worship at the Servite Church in Florence. They also followed a strict regime of fasting, and went out of their way to help the poor. They always dressed in simple black clothing hoping to witness against the opulent and showy manner in which the wealthy women of Florence dressed. Juliana became the leader of the Marian Sisters of her time. She led them in prayer, in penance and in service. When Juliana's life was drawing

Painting over Main Altar in Servite Basilica.
Blessed Mother appears every First Saturday.

to a close, she wanted to receive Communion one last time. Since she was so weak, she could not receive our Lord in the Eucharist. The priest placed the host over her heart which was quite common during the Middle Ages for those who could no longer swallow the host. After placing the host on her heart, the priest prayed that God, who had placed the soul in the body, would sanctify the sick person through the Body of Christ. After the host was placed on Juliana's heart, her face beamed with delight. She died in peace, and it was noted that the host was nowhere to be found. It was apparent that Juliana's desire to receive the Eucharist had been granted to her. She died in 1341, and Pope Clement XII canonized her in 1737.

Over the main altar in the Servite Basilica in Chicago, there is a huge painting of a scene I just described. Every first Saturday while praying the Seven Dolor Rosary, the Blessed Mother and the Child Jesus appear in that painting very clearly for most people to see. The people who have seen Mary and the Child Jesus report that she appears in a shaft of light, and is holding the Child Jesus while keeping Her eyes fixed on the Eucharist. Juliana has been revered as the "Saint of the Eucharist." The Servite Sisters wear the host upon their habit to remember that they are in a special way dedicated to the Eucharist. I always like to have a healing service in a special way dedicated to the Eucharist. If possible, I like to have the laying on of the hands in the presence of Our Lord exposed in the Blessed Sacrament. I also take the Monstrance with the Eucharist in it and bless the seriously ill. At the end, I have Benediction for all present. Juliana's relic is in my Crucifix which I use to bless those present. She is associated with many

St. Anthony Pucci

thousands and thousands of healings. You know, Margaret, as I was going through Juliana's life, I could not help but see a parallel to your life as the Foundress of Mary's Helpers. She came from a very wealthy family, and you, Margaret, were a very successful clothing and costume designer who came from rather comfortable circumstances. I believe you decided to go the same route as Saint Juliana. She eventually asked for the habit of the Servite Order while adopting a very simple way of life as well as dress.

(M) Until today, I did not know much about Saint Juliana's life. However, I too, can see the parallel in some ways. When I began to do Our Lady's work, I realized I was being called away from wearing the beautiful dresses I always wore. By Mary calling me to a simpler life, I changed to white shirts, black skirts, black jackets, and a white and blue neck scarf tied into a bow. In fact, my shoes are pretty much the same as the ones worn by the nuns. Since that time, many of Mary's Helpers are now doing the same thing. About a year ago, I was called to wear this all the time. Yes, Father, I see the parallel.

(F) I always enjoy talking about the Servite saints because they are so inspiring.

(M) Father, tell us about St. Anthony Pucci.

(F) Saint Anthony Pucci is a rather recent saint who was canonized at the opening session of Vatican II by Pope John XXIII as a model for the fathers of the council. His life can be used as a model to everyone that we can all become saints. Anthony was very ordinary. It is very difficult to find any great thing that he did or any gift he possessed. Anthony never underestimated the significance of anything he did in God's service.

Anthony, small in stature and very timid, did not look like a leader or sound like one. In fact, he had an unpleasant speaking voice, and had great difficulty giving a talk unless he memorized it. Any public confrontation made him extremely uncomfortable especially if it was over politics or religion. Because he truly gave himself to God, he found himself doing things that people like him would not normally do. As pastor in Viareggio, God brought Anthony to heights he did not expect. In the 1800s, Viareggio was a simple fishing village on the Mediterranean with its inhabitants loyal to the Catholic faith. While Anthony was stationed there, the simple, basic life began to change. The wealthy people from the cities began vacationing at the town's beaches. These vacationers brought their own kind of entertainment and it was something completely new to the villagers. The quiet little village was turned up side down, especially with the anti-Church attitude which was springing up among the leaders of the town. The members of the community who wanted to get ahead politically found it advantageous to reject the Church and its beliefs. During these troubled times, Anthony simply fulfilled the duties of a parish priest as well as he could. He dedicated his parish to Our Lady of Sorrows, and urged his parishioners to make their faith visible by displaying Mary's image on their boats and in their homes. Anthony organized religion classes for everyone of all ages, and encouraged his parishioners to perform acts of charity. He did this so the local political leaders could not claim that the Church was not interested in its citizenry. Part of his ministry was to make daily visits to the shut-ins.

Anthony was a peacemaker for his parishioners, and he spent long hours in the confessional. He never rushed any sacramental celebration or took any celebration lightly. He lovingly spent hours guiding, counseling, and sharing with his congregation the Lord's gift of forgiveness. He practiced what he preached and he was a man of great integrity. Anthony's death came partially as a result of his giving his coat to a poor man who had none in the middle of the winter.

As you can see, he did nothing dazzling, but, in his own way, he rebuilt the town in which he lived. He credited his daily prayer life for giving him the strength to do what he had to do in order to keep his town from becoming a den of iniquity. Anthony was the most respected man in town by the time he died in 1892. On the day of his funeral, all work stopped so that everyone could attend the funeral Mass. The anti-clerical town politicians had been won over, and they declared the day a holiday.

You know, Margaret, Maria Valtora, the author of **The Poem the Man God** lived in Viareggio. I feel that it was the beautiful spiritual atmosphere created by Saint Anthony Pucci that helped inspire her to write this great work. She was a very saintly person who was a victim soul because she suffered terribly in her life. The later part of her life was a life of severe physical suffering. In fact, most of the time Maria wrote from her sick bed on the insistence of her spiritual director, Father Minorini. Father Derti was also closely associated with Maria. He was a great Marian Theologian from our facility in the Marianno in Rome. He was a saintly man. I knew him very well.

(M) This is a wonderful testimony about a priest who lived his life just wanting to be a good parish priest and living the Word of God.

(F) God chooses the least among us.

(M) We have with us today, Father Peter Mary Rookey. He is from Chicago, and he has been in the healing ministry for over forty three years. It is good to have you with us once again, Father

(F) Thank you, Margaret. It is always a joy to be with you, and I feel privileged to be invited by you to speak about our Servite saints. Today, I am going to speak about the latest one to be canonized, Saint Clelia Barbieri.

(M) Earlier, you were telling me a little bit about her, and it sounds like her life was extremely interesting even though not a lot was said about her.

(F) Except for Saint Peregrine, the Cancer Saint, most of the Servite saints, like their Foundress, Mary, are very humble and not as well known as some of the greater saints. They followed in Her humility. We know very little about the life of Mary except through private revelations. Saint Clelia is no exception. Do you have any questions?

(M) No, Father, go on. If something comes up, I will ask you.

(F) You are welcome to interrupt me at any time. In fact, I welcome interruptions, especially if they are questions that would elaborate on a point that I had skimmed over.

St. Clelia Barbieri

Clelia Barbieri was born in Bologna, Italy, on February 13, 1847 of a very poor family. She was so poor that when she was called to the religious life, she was afraid no religious institute would have her. In the days of Clelia, when a young lady wanted to become a religious, she would have to be provided with a dowry that usually came from her family or a benefactor. At that time, a dowry was a sum of money given to the religious community to enable the young lady to enter the order, and to provide for her education as well as her training. Many religious orders depended on the dowry, because they had no other means of remuneration. Some orders had hospitals or schools to run. Therefore, they needed the incomes from the dowries to keep them open because they had no other or very few avenues of income. Clelia's father died when she was eight or nine years of age, and her mother struggled to support her family by sewing and weaving. From her mother, Clelia learned some of the simple arts. You, Margaret, are a person who started out sewing like Clelia.

(M) Yes. I also started at an early age. I was eight years old when I made my first dress, and my mother was so proud of me. I even made the button holes all by myself. We had a grocery store, and she would show it to everyone who came into the store. I remember it so well. It was blue with little red roses.

(F) Therefore, Margaret you can relate to little Clelia. She learned the art of surviving on very little from her mother. Her mother taught her to sew, cook, scrimp, save, and make ends meet.

(M) That was the same way with my family, Father. I am one of nine children, and my mother had to do the same things as Clelia's mother in order to help my father support our family.

(F) Clelia learned atonement. Family prayer and Sunday Mass was part of their life no matter what else happened. She would go to vespers on Sunday evening, and afterwards, she and three of her friends would meet to talk about their faith as well as their experiences in prayer. The time they would spend together was the high point of their week, and it went by all too quickly. All four of these young ladies felt a calling to the religious life. Because, they were all so poor, they did not think any religious order would take them. It was at this time that they began to think about creating a community themselves. The pastor of their parish church must have been a very holy man, because he invited them to move into a small dwelling called the House of the Master. This is how they began.

(M) They did not have anyone to teach them?

(F) They were near Bologna where there are many Servites who have been there since the earliest years of the Order. It was this group of Servites who fostered this devotion in them. Clelia became the superior.

(M) How old was she at the time?

(F) Clelia was twenty-one years of age at the time. She wrote a short Rule of Life for this community which stressed prayer, sacrifice, work and love. However, Clelia was already in the early stages of tuberculosis, and she was confined to bed for seven months. She died at the age of twenty-three on July 13, 1870.

The group she founded became known as The Little Sisters of the Sorrowful Mother. Minims was the popular name for their Order or their congregation. The Minims aggregated to the Servite family in 1951 as sisters. Clelia was beatified by Pope Paul VI in 1968, and her body is venerated in the chapel at the congregation motherhouse in LaBoudru. Our present Holy Father, Pope John Paul II, canonized her. She lived a very short life, and moved up into the ranks of Sainthood in a very short time.

The community that she founded took as a special apostolate the care of orphaned and abandoned girls. Her community gave these girls training in the domestic arts, and the practice of the Catholic faith. Clelia grew rapidly in the intensity of her prayer life. In her letter to Jesus, Clelia wrote, "Oh Great God, You see my constant longing to love You and never to displease You. Lord, open Your heart of love that I may be consumed with a little love." As Clelia grew in holiness, she grew physically weaker. Her last words to her community were, "Be a good cheer. I'm going to paradise, but I'll always be with you, and never desert you." Please bid adieu to this beautiful short lived saint who conquered much in a short time, Saint Clelia Barberi. I would like to remark at this time that there are so many great saints that did so much in a very few years. Saint Therese, the Little Flower, was a contemporary of Clelia. She died at twenty-four, and she did so much in those few years. Therese is still powerful, to this day, with us and the Lord. Saint Anthony of Padua died in his late twenties, and Saint Francis of Assisi was in his forties when he passed away. So many of the great saints had very short lives, and yet they accomplished worlds of good in those short years.

(M) Father, thanks again, and how about a blessing for our listening audience.

(F) I have a relic of Saint Clelia in my hand, and I bless you. The blessings of God which know neither time nor space goes out to you from here. "Through the prayers and merits of Our Blessed Lady, Saint Clelia Barbieri, and all the Servite saints, may the blessing of Almighty God, the Father, Son, and Holy Spirit descend upon you and heal you, remaining with you forever. Amen."

(M) Thank you so much, Father. God bless you, and I hope you, the listening audience have enjoyed this beautiful prayer from Father Rookey.

(F) I hope I can come back to you again with more of the charisma of the Servite Order.

(M) Thank you so much, Father Peter Mary Rookey.

FATHER SPEAKS ABOUT MARRIAGE AND DIVORCE

The following interview is taken from a radio program with Father Peter Mary Rookey, O.S.M. and Margaret Trosclair on October 8, 1995.

(M) Father, so many people are having problems with marriage and are divorcing. They are not realizing what is happening in their lives. Many are not being healed. Many don't know how to get out of the web they have weaved. I think you are the person that can help these people.

(F) I know very often when people come to be healed, they don't realize their outlook and relationship with God is not right. They cannot be healed.

What comes to mind immediately is a young man in Holy Ghost Church in London, about five years ago, who had AIDS. It was very embarrassing for the young man's father. I told him, "If you want to be healed, you have to promise the Lord that you will not carry out this form of life, living as a homosexual. This is a very serious sin against marriage." He promised and he was healed instantly. This was in many papers. It was written up and his doctors attested to his healing.

We must become right with the Lord, and then we are able to be healed. In fact, that is a healing. Of course, the inner healing is always the greatest healing and the lasting one. This is so important, that is why I use this example often.

I'm going to recommend to you that we take up one of the most important documents that has come out in recent years, and maybe centuries, and that is the Catechism of the Catholic Church which goes into detail about many of the questions on our mind, including all the questions surrounding marriage or the abuse of marriage. You will find a quick synthesis in the catechism from which we are quoting today. You'll find it in the paragraph numbers. The book is very beautifully and practically set up with the paragraphs with numbers. You can quickly find in the index what you are looking for. We are quoting today the part on marriage which is summed up in numbers 1659 to 1666. This catechism is a best seller. The marriage covenant which a man and a woman form with each other, an intimate communion of life and love was founded and endowed with its own special laws by the Creator. By its very nature marriage is ordered to the good of the couple as well as the generation and education of children. Christ, our Lord, raised marriage between baptized persons to the dignity of a Sacrament. That is, He made it an outward sign that gives a special grace. This is quite a different thing from signing an agreement before a Justice of the Peace, which is a legal agreement. This is a Sacrament. We make this agreement promising not only ourselves, but promising God in His sight and calling upon Him. What we are doing is what we intend. It is very serious and solemn.

(M) Many people do not take marriage so seriously. It is for better or for worse. They forget about these serious vows.

(F) I believe we can trace the lack of seriousness to total rejection. In the Sixteenth Century of the Rock, Peter, as represented by the Holy Father, when the Real Presence of Christ in the Sacrament of the Eucharist was rejected during the reformation, the other sacraments, which gain their power from the Eucharist, lost their importance. These sacraments are the doing, you could say, of the life, passion, death and resurrection of Christ's life. When the consecration was dismissed as simply a ceremony, the other sacraments fell, too, because they obtain their power from the life, death and resurrection of Jesus. When the Sacrament of Marriage was no longer regarded as a sacrament, but just simply a ceremony, divorce became very easy. It was not all that serious. It was looked upon as a contract, where the two parties making the contract could decide to break it. If you and I are in partnership in a business and we decide to go our own ways, we legally dissolve that partnership.

(M) This is where the problem is coming in now. Couples think that they can go on and marry again, and maybe the next one they marry may not have been married.

(F) This is a complete attack by satan. It is so fundamental in our society and he knows that. He has made it all a joke, instead of allowing us to be enriched and strengthened by the power of this Sacrament and be faithful to our commitment before God. It is a satanic attack on the whole world against the foundation stone of our society.

(M) When a person who was never married before, marries a divorced person, he or she loses all rights in the Church. Is that correct?

(F) They divorce themselves from the Church.

(M) Even though these persons have gotten a divorce, they are living an adulterous life?

(F) In the eyes of the Church, when you divorce from your spouse, you are declaring that Christ's teaching about marriage is nothing, and has no value. In effect, you are separating from Christ and His Church.

(M) In plain words, you make the choice. You are either for God or against God. You are divorcing yourself from the Church and from Christ. People do not realize this and are living in sin. This is why many people are not being healed, and they need to get out of this situation. How can they get out of this situation, Father?

(F) First, you have to see what situation they are in. If they have been divorced by their spouse, even against their will, they are still held as a Christian.

(M) The party that is wanting the divorce is the offender. That is on his soul.

(F) At the same time, we are not estimating the sorrow and the stress and pain attached to such things. That is what makes divorce a great evil. We are not even touching on the effects of the children. We are poisoning the poor children. We are depriving the children of a father or a mother. In many cases, when there are several attempted marriages after the first valid marriage, the children are completely in chaos. They don't know where they are. They have no mother or father.

(M) Father, that goes to show you what's happening with the children. Parents don't realize that this is some of the reason why children are going into drugs or whatever.

(F) It's a lack of love. Children think, "When I am not loved by my own parents, who can I trust?" We often say about the unborn child that when it is aborted or unwanted, it leaves a mark on the child, even in the womb. Doctors have told us that whether the father and mother want the child or not, it leaves a mark on the child. If the child is unwanted, it carries over into adulthood and into their marriage.

In the old testament, polygamy in the mosaic law was allowed. That was in putting away my wife. In the old testament, Our Lord said it was because of the hardness of their hearts. God made them male and female. What God has joined let no man put asunder. So, unity and unbreakableness of that bond is called indissolubility. Openness to use our marriage rights to bring about unity is essential to marriage. Divorce separates what God has joined together. The refusal to have children turns married life away from the supreme gift of marriage, which is to have children.

The following interview is taken from a radio program with Father Peter Mary Rookey, O.S.M. and Margaret Trosclair on October 15, 1995.

(M) Our guest today is Father Peter Mary Rookey, O.S.M. who was with us last week. His talk on marriage was beautifully done. I'm sure many of you have questions that need to be answered. We hope that in some way, through the talk Father will give today, you will be helped to overcome some of the fears you have in your marriage, how to get along with your spouse, and to accept the things that may be happening. When a couple takes their vows, it is for better or worse. If we want to get better in our lives and other situations, we need to realize that being in the predicament, we feel we are in, sometimes stops us from really loving our spouse as we should. Is that correct, Father?

(F) In the ministry of healing it will certainly obstruct our healing when we are not in tune with the Lord, when we are not living His Good News. He has given us such Good News in the Gospels.

(M) Father, I sometimes think about young couples who are in love and want to marry. I know that two people can fall out of love just as quickly as they can fall into love, due to various circumstances at the time. However, I believe, if they just sit and talk out their problems, they can work them out.

(F) I think the difficulty comes from the understanding of love. We understand love as mostly our feelings, but love is an act of an individual's will. Let us say that I am married to a beautiful blonde, and, because of an accident, she becomes disfigured. Now, she is not so beautiful and I am no longer attracted to her body. Maybe she becomes an invalid and I don't love her anymore. As you can see, my love for her came from her physical beauty.

Love is centered in the individual's will, and this is the love God has for us. He shares His love with us. If my love is only a love of physical attraction, or other qualities I see in another person, it is a come and go kind of love. When these things cease, many people say they are leaving the other one because they don't love the other person any longer. They don't love their spouse any more because they have seen someone else who has the physical qualities they want to see in their spouse. As Jesus said, and Paul repeats after Him, "We love to the end."

We must use whatever means is necessary to overcome any problems we might have with our spouse. Even when someone goes against us we must reach out to that person. We cannot remove a person from our life because of trouble or difficulty. We must love in spite of everything, and this is true love of the will. If our love is only on the surface, we are in trouble. Divorce, which is contrary to Christ's laws, has become too easy. In Chicago, attorneys are advertising divorces for $250.00. I guess you could say it is comparable to getting out of the water by jumping into the fire.

Some people are divorced against their will. They, of course, are not allowed to marry again because, in the eyes of the Church, the first marriage is forever. When a couple gets married, they are asking God to witness their vows. They are asking Him to witness as to the truth of what they are saying. The couple intends to carry out these vows. Attempted remarriage of persons divorced from a living, lawful spouse contravenes a law and a plan that God has taught through Christ, "What God has joined, let no one put asunder." The couple separates themselves from the Eucharist, because they cannot receive Christ into their body and soul. The person, or persons, is no longer living or showing his love for Christ. He or she is going against what He tells them. Jesus said, "You love Me if you keep my commandments." If we do not keep His commandments, we cannot be in communion with Him. That is why people who are living outside the laws of Christ cut themselves off from Christ. If a divorced person would receive communion, it would be an insult to Christ because that person is not following Him.

(M) Of course, the person being divorced against his or her will can go to communion.

(F) Of course, if they are not guilty. Marriage is for life, and according to Christ's law, they cannot remarry. (We call it remarriage.) Christ said, "Till death do us part." Love is the greatest power in the universe. It is even greater than the most terrible bomb that man can create. The power of love is what brings us to love to the end, or until death do us part. The couple stands before the altar and pledges to one another their devotion, in sickness and health, poverty and riches, until death.

I would like to talk about some of the abuses attacking the sacrament of marriage. The basic law is love of God and love of our neighbor. In creating the human being, man and woman, God gives personal dignity equally to each one. Man and woman should acknowledge and accept his or her special sexual identity. Christ is the model of chastity. Every baptized person is called to live a chaste life according to the personal state of life he or she is living at the time. If a person is married, he or she must live chastely in the marriage. Couples must avoid anything that may destroy their love for each other. Chastity means that our sexuality is an integrated one within our person. We must train ourselves to live a life according to God's chaste law.

(M) Many people who have committed adultery in their marriage are very sorry for their actions. However, they do not realize that they must confess this to unburden themselves in order to be healed.

(F) That is why God gave us the sacrament of Confession.

(M) Everyone needs to know how to come to grips with these problems. They can go to their pastor, priest or spiritual director because he is bound to secrecy. Whatever he is told, must remain between the two of them and God. The priest, who represents God, is bound not to tell anything that is told to him. There are times when everyone has to unload their problems. If anyone needs to do this, do it now. Now is the time to rid yourself of all the things that have been bothering you. Also, make amends with God.

(F) Love is the love of God, and God's love is unchangeable. God's love is everlasting. Whenever we turn to Him, we can be absolved from our sins. Among the sins gravely contrary to chastity, whether we are single or married, are masturbation, fornication, pornography and homosexual practices. The covenant, which man and woman make in their marriage, brings the obligation of indissolubility, the unbreakableness of that bond we make. Some people get carried away in their great desire to overcome the abuses of alcohol and drugs by declaring that drugs and alcohol are evil. Everything God created is good. Marriage is good and having children is a great good. Where would we be without this act of marriage? To condemn something because it is abused is wrong. A couple must not regulate the number of their children by going against God's law. Sterilization and contraception are not according to God's law. Also, abortion is a terrible evil. Trial marriage, adultery, divorce, polygamy, sins of all kinds against children, and free unions are grave offenses against the dignity of the sacrament of Marriage.

TESTIMONIES

The following are testimonies of healings received during healing services conducted by Father Peter Mary Rookey:

Dearest Father Rookey,

We sent you a picture of our unborn baby son, and asked for your prayers. We hoped he would be born without the disease the doctors had diagnosed.

Our son was born December 12, and, on December 13, we found out that he did not have polycystic kidney disease, but just enlarged kidneys. He is perfectly healthy. We definitely know our son is truly a miracle baby. We can't thank you enough for all your prayers and concerns during our time of need.

Thanks again and God bless you.

KANSAS CITY, MO

Dear Father Rookey,

Thank you so much for your letter, newsletter and your book. I was happy to hear from you.

I have a daughter who is a nurse in a children's hospital. One night she rang me very excited. She said, "I have great news about Father Rookey." She went on to tell me about the young boy in a coma, brain damaged for months. There was no hope from the doctors. They said he would die.

She said, "Father Rookey came in, prayed over the boy, and he was healed. He is now at home." She was very excited when I had told her how I witnessed the healing of the young nurse in Medjugorje. Praise the Lord!

May God and our Blessed Lady keep you safe and bless you always in your good work.

IRELAND

Dear Father Rookey,

When my son Rick was eighteen months old he was diagnosed with a brain tumor. In February, 1989, he had his first surgery, and then chemotherapy. In September, 1989 his tumor was back. They operated again and told us radiation was our only hope. However, the doctors didn't think it would work. Richie was unable to eat, walk, or talk. In January 1990, we went to see you at Saint Clare Church and you blessed him. About two weeks later Richie told us Mary talked to him and said she was going to take his tumor away. That kept our spirit up.

He went for a test in March, and his tumor had shrunk. In July 1990, Richie had his third surgery. Before his surgery, his father and I told God that "His Will be done." We would understand whatever the outcome. Richie's surgery went well, and it was not a tumor but a cyst. We felt the Lord tested us and we passed.

Richie is very special. He is responsible for bringing our entire family back to Church. Even his doctors and nurses are praying. They feel Richie is with us because of the "Power of Prayer."

OHIO

Dear Father Rookey,

I don't know if you remember me, but I had a healing in June 1991, in Medjugorje. Through the power of Christ, you were the priest who healed me. Upon my arrival, I was in a wheelchair until you prayed over me.

I was examined by my doctors for the first time yesterday, and they found very few signs of Multiple Sclerosis, but they would not declare a miracle. They couldn't answer my question as to why I suddenly walked after three and a half years, but just claimed I'm in remission! Nevertheless, I'm still giving testimony. I know something special happened to me.

I spend my days caring for my friends with Multiple Sclerosis. I visit those confined to nursing homes. The ones who are mobile, I take out. I feel this is my calling since Our Lord blessed me. Thank you again for your help in my healing.

RHODE ISLAND

Father Peter Rookey,

In December I attended the healing Mass and prayed for vision so I could see faces. I am blind, but my prayer was for my ability to see a face. When I looked at you, I could see you.

My eye doctor told me on the 18th of December that my left eye looks very optimistic. From time to time I can now see the faces of those I love. Father, this is a miracle. I am very grateful to you and to God.

FLORIDA

Dear Father Rookey,

I heard about you through a friend of a man with whom I work. In March 1991, I had no idea I had a health problem.

All I knew was that I had developed a swollen abdomen which made me look like I was nine months pregnant. I thought I was just overweight. However, tests showed a definite large growth, and an operation was advised.

On March 28, I had exploratory surgery. On March 29, I was told I had a malignant sarcoma of the abdomen which was too extensive to be operable. I was assigned a doctor who said he didn't think radiation or chemotherapy would do much good. On May 14, I flew to London to get more information about you, Father Rookey. The Lord sent you my way through friends. A man who had heard about my cancer thought perhaps you could help me to change my mind about giving up. I flew to Ohio, and had the most wonderful spiritual weekend of my life. I took part in your healing Masses on June 7, 8, and 9. My faith was renewed, and replenished during this weekend. Physically, I felt better every day, and I was able to move around more freely. It was a most remarkable weekend, and I felt blessed. Hundreds and hundreds of people who attended your healing Masses prayed for me. I felt extremely positive, and I knew I was not fighting the battle with cancer alone.

I never had a single negative thought from the time I left London, until the time I admitted myself into the hospital for the surgery. The aorta did not have to be resected, and surgery, which could have taken up to twelve hours, took only four. The surgeon removed close to ten pounds of tumor and fluid from my body. Following the surgery, I spent thirty days in the hospital. I never felt anything but a positive attitude as well as a wonderful feeling of being glad to be alive. I know that Jesus and Our Lady were with me every step of the way.

Thank you, Father Rookey, for your healing Masses and the spiritual energy they gave to me. I pray that you continue

God's work for many, many years to come. May Mary bless you.

NEW YORK

Dear Father Rookey,

My story is very involved, and I am writing to you to let you know that I have truly been touched by Jesus.

For two years, I had suffered from tremendous head pain. I finally found a doctor who would listen, and would hang in there with me. My doctor ordered a MRI which showed a shadow that doctors thought was a vascular mass. They ordered an arteriography which showed I had a small benign tumor.

The surgeon who was called in on my case told me I would probably not survive the surgery. The least I could hope for was to be blind and paralyzed, or I could end up in a vegetative state. Arrangements were made for me to be in the hospital twelve to fourteen weeks, and then go to a re-hab center. Breaking the news to my two small children was frightening.

Before surgery, the doctors became very angry with me. I told them Jesus would not desert me, and that I would be fine. They told us that the surgery would be about three hours; however, it ended up being seven and one-half hours. When the doctors opened me up, they realized I should have been dead months before. My brain was starting to disintegrate because it was so swollen. The tumor was twice the size shown on the test. Plus, it was wrapped around the brain stem. The doctors were astounded that I could talk, recognize people, or wiggle my fingers and toes.

I was on the critical list for three days. Unknown to me, at the time, you came in. My girlfriend had gone to see you, and told you she had a friend who just underwent brain surgery. She told you we did not know if it was cancerous. You told her it was, but that I would be cured. She then stood in proxy for me. She said, before she went down, her head burned, and it felt like it had cracked in three places. The places she felt crack were the same three places where I was cut. You told her to go to the hospital, lay her hands on my head, and say the **Miracle Prayer**. She did as you said, and I took a turn for the better the next day. I was out of Neuro in a week and a half. I am fine today.

I wanted to take this opportunity to thank you for helping to cure and heal me through the help of Jesus. I end this letter to you in the way I end all of my prayers daily.

"May Jesus forever live in my heart, be the sounds in my ears, the words on my lips and the lamplight of my eyes."

OHIO

Dear Father Rookey

As I entered the room for our Spiritual Life Committee meeting at the parish, I was stopped by a couple. They went on to tell me that their friend from Texas was diagnosed with brain cancer. They told her to go to the Cleveland Clinic to see if anything could be done for her. This is the reason why she was at your healing service. The doctors at the clinic told her to return home, and to begin chemotherapy. There was nothing that could be done for her.

After the Mass and healing service, the woman returned home. When more tests and x-rays of her head were taken, all traces of cancer were gone. Thanks be to God. Praise You, Jesus!

In the love of Our Most Loving Mother and Savior Jesus Christ.

OHIO

Dear Fr. Rookey,

I've carried your **Miracle Prayer** card in my wallet since you gave the healing service at our Church in the fall or near Christmas time, 1991. Seeing your picture reminds me of what my husband and I came for that night, and how our prayers were answered. In May of last year, my husband was diagnosed with terminal lung cancer.

One of my prayers that night was for my husband's physical healing. I also prayed for a spiritual healing for him, and for our family. We have five children ages ten to twenty. Nothing spectacular happened right off. We spoke to you before we left the hall and I felt satisfied that we'd done what God required of us. I know you realize how hard it is for sick people to come and sit for a long time. He was very tired when we drove home

As he was dying, the miracle happened, and he made his peace with everyone close to him. As I brought the children in to see him, I felt the joy and peace of family healing. The memory of this will always be a comfort to me. The last thing he said was, "I love you."

God left the family a wonderful gift of healing and peace. Even after seven months, it has helped us bear the burden of grief that still come in waves.

Thank you again, Father. I'll always remember you.

MAINE

Dear Father Rookey,

I am the organist at my Church, but I was ready to quit this position. I also thought about closing my piano tuning business due to two different types of arthritis in my hands as well as severe deterioration of the bone in my left wrist. I had great difficulty dressing myself, doing normal household chores, and driving a car. Playing the organ or servicing pianos was almost impossible. I suffered a great deal of pain, especially in the left wrist. I was unable to lift anything or wear a watch on my left wrist. No pain-killing medication would help or relieve the pain.

I was wearing braces on both wrists so I could play for the Healing Mass on October 26, 1992. Even though I wasn't feeling well, I was more concerned about my daughter and granddaughter. Both my daughter and granddaughter suffered injuries from an auto accident which occurred before the baby's birth. They were present for the healing service.

When you touched me, my pain immediately and thoroughly disappeared. I took the braces off, and was able to totally move all my fingers. I could even make a fist and squeeze everyone's hand. I could pick up my music case, and my heavy books without any difficulty or pain. I was even able to hold my baby granddaughter for the first time. To this day, I have been using my hands, fingers, and arms as if nothing has ever been wrong. Now, I bowl, pick up grocery bags, and dress myself. I play the organ and piano better than ever before.

Praise God! I owe Him everything!

ILLINOIS

Dear Father Rookey,

Jesus says that all who come to Him will have healing as long as they have faith. Through the Name of Jesus, you were used to heal my son. For eight years, he had severe schizophrenia. The doctors told him he would have to live with this illness. Every year, he went into the hospital. Even though it made me sad to see my son deteriorate, I never gave up. When he came to you on May 23, he was healed completely. There were signs and wonders. He is now laughing, and keeping himself clean. There is no more confusion, and no more fear.

I could not walk, and had spinal problems. My right leg was two inches shorter than my left, but now it is even. After you prayed for me in Jesus' Name, I was healed.

Yours in Christ!

LONDON

Dear Father Rookey,

I had to write and tell you about the blessing God has given me. He led me to you for my son. At the time, I had no knowledge of your gifts. When invited by a friend to go to your healing service and Mass, we went.

At this time, my son, had an immune deficiency, and, most of all, a bizarre behavior problem. We attended the Mass even though it was difficult because of my son's behavior. By the time I coaxed him down to the altar, I was a total wreck. You blessed my son, and when you blessed me, the Holy Spirit was so strong I could feel the peace of God with me. When I woke up, I experienced a beautiful peace. I had no idea that God was giving me the strength for what was to come.

After a few weeks, my son's behavior got worse. It was almost like he was demonic. The fear inside me grew. I knew there was something else wrong with my child. I had gone to several types of doctors, psychiatrists and pediatricians, but no one could tell me why my son acted as he did. Through a lot of searching and praying, my son was admitted to Children's Hospital where he underwent several tests. When the neurologist ordered a MRI, a tumor was discovered. It covered the whole right side of his brain. Finally, his behavior was explained. Later, a biopsy was taken, and the neurologist told me it was malignant. However, they did not know its type.

I kept praying all the time, and I felt I had nothing left to give. We stayed in the hospital for over a month. One afternoon, the neurologist came into our room, and told me the tumor was not malignant after all. He told us we could go home, but we were to return every three months for a checkup.

It has been almost a year, and the tumor has not enlarged. My son has never received any treatment except for the immune deficiency. His behavior is not normal, but is a lot better than before the surgery.

As I look back, I know that God sent me to that Mass, and I marvel at how God works. There is no doubt in my mind that the healing for my son's tumor was received at that Mass. I thank God for using you as His instrument, and I thank you for your prayers.

Thank you, Blessed Mother, for your intercession.

LOUISIANA

Dear Father Rookey,

This is a testimony of a healing that I received through you when you came to a Day of Renewal in London, 1991.

I suffered a heart attack in July 1990, and was admitted to the hospital. After many tests, I was told that I had two blocked arteries, and would have to have a double by-pass operation. In September 1990, I was told that I would have to wait about six months before the operation could be performed.

A few weeks before I was due for tests prior to having the operation, I met you at the Day of Renewal. I told you about my problem, and you prayed over me for some minutes. As you prayed, I was filled with a lovely coolness. I cannot describe it in any other way. At the same time, a tremendous force was pushing me to the ground. I knew that I had been healed. I would like to add here that this was the very first time I had every been to a healing service. Even though I had only been attending the Day of Renewal for a few months, I did not know anything about you at all.

When I was eventually called to the hospital for the necessary tests, my doctor could not believe the results. He asked me what I had been doing? At this point, it was quite clear that I would not now need the surgery. He asked me if I was still taking the prescribed medication, and I told him "No." I had not taken any medication since you prayed over me.

He had me back again later in the same year for more tests. "Just in case," he said. He still could not understand what happened, and seemed reluctant to discharge me. However, I went back again in November, 1991, and this time, I was officially discharged.

I thank God for sending me to that healing service and for the healing He gave me through you.

ENGLAND

Healing Priest Performs Unscheduled "Exorcism"
by Don Meehan

I had never been to a healing Mass, much less an exorcism. As I stood there watching this beautiful outpouring of unselfish and generous love coming from the priest and the forty witnesses to this poor helpless soul, I realized that I was witnessing an event that so few on this planet had ever seen or ever will see. There wasn't a camera or a recorder anywhere to record it for the world to see and hear. I couldn't sleep that night thinking that I must do everything possible to remember what had happened and write it down to the best of my ability.

An impromptu, unscheduled and unplanned "exorcism" was performed after a healing Mass led by an internationally known healing priest at Our Lady of Mount Carmel Church in Doylestown, Pennsylvania, on the night of January 20, 1992.

Over fourteen hundred people had attended a "healing Mass" conducted by Father Peter Mary Rookey, a Servite priest from Chicago, and most all of them had received from him the special blessing known as "laying on of the hands." After the services, a young man began yelling and screaming violently and acting strange and had to be held down on the altar by at least four strong men. The paramedics were called but soon realized that they really couldn't be of any help, for the man was apparently "possessed" by an evil spirit.

Father Rookey was preparing to leave, when someone summoned him to come and "do something." He hurried back to the altar and put the same Cross he had used for the healings in front of the young man's face. He screamed, he growled, he snarled and spat on the priest and the Cross as at least forty people watched helplessly. The priest was now convinced that the man was taken over by an evil spirit.

Father Rookey then began to exorcise Frankie (not his real name, but we'll call him Frankie to protect his privacy), using his Cross containing relics of the Saints and Blessed of his Order of the Servite Fathers, holy water and blessed oil and the prescribed exorcism prayers of the Catholic Church. The alleged demonic activity was similar to what was shown in the movie, "The Exorcist," only now it was really unfolding right before our eyes. Not one of the forty worshipers left the man's side. They stayed there until the very end, praying every prayer they knew over Frankie.

The man, allegedly possessed by an evil spirit, or a demon, snarled and growled and spat upon the priest and the Cross and others around him. He stuck his tongue way out in a point an shook it. He could not even bear to look at the Cross. He screamed out things like: "Get that man away from me. Get that Cross away from me. I hate Him." He spat again and again on the priest and the Cross, and screamed and growled and twisted his face and body into terrible contortions, rolled his eyes and crossed them repeatedly, and stuck his tongue out and shook it violently like a snake. The face, especially the eyes and the mouth, was a picture of hatred. Then there were moments when Frankie appeared to be in control and would say in his normal soft and gentle voice: "What's happening to me?" "I'm sorry for this." "Am I going to die?" And he would burst into tears. And then the tongue would go out again, the eyes would roll, the voice would change and the demon apparently would take control again.

It all began when at least a hundred and fifty or more persons out of the more than fourteen hundred who had received the "laying on of the hands," received the "gift" that Catholics call "resting in the Spirit." To describe it briefly, after the "laying on of the (healing) hands" some recipients will just collapse into the arms of a "catcher," who is positioned behind the recipient to gently let the person go down flat on his back. It is similar to fainting, except that the person retains consciousness and is aware of what is going on around him. Catholics believe that the Holy Spirit actually takes over the person's faculties at that time. It generally lasts from a few seconds to over a half hour or longer. Frankie was among those who "rested in the Spirit" but failed to come out of it and became violent.

The exorcism went on for at least two hours with the forty witnesses saying every prayer they knew, and bringing out relics, medals, crosses and rosaries, including a gold turned one from Medjugorje, the now famous village of the on-going ten year old apparitions of the Virgin Mary in Yugoslavia. One lady had a relic of Padre Pio, the famous stigmata priest, and a man even had a mixture of holy waters from Medjugorje, Lourdes, Fatima and the Jordan River where the Bible says that Jesus was baptized. The alleged demon seemed to suffer the most when Father Rookey poured the holy water into the man's mouth and on him, and put his Cross in front of his face. Catholic literature claims that the Cross, or Crucifix, and the Name of Jesus spoken, is most terrifying to an evil spirit. It also states that "Sacramentals and blessed objects are also effective remedies." However, there appeared to be a turning point when Father Rookey took the Medjugorje rosary and touched it to the man's head, throat and lips, and called on the "Lady of Medjugorje" to expel the demon. All of the forty witnesses joined him in chorus.

After about two hours the alleged demon apparently gave up and left the man's body. Frankie, totally exhausted, was finally able to stand up and leave the altar. Father Rookey said later the "possession" occurs often after a healing service and recommended that Frankie attend another healing Mass the next evening and attempt to locate an exorcist in the Archdiocese to continue the prescribed prayers. He told about a case where a lady was infected with five demons and he was able to identify only one who said he was Lucifer, and that it took a year for exorcists to expel the demons.

The Church early instituted the Order of Exorcist and later composed formulas of prayers to be employed by those in the exercise of their office. Since the office is an extremely difficult one and presupposes much knowledge, virtue and tact, its solemn exercise has been restricted to priests expressly deputed for that purpose.

According to some sources it is difficult to obtain an exorcism in the United States. One author states: "It's unfortunate, but in the United States we have to go through a lot of red tape to get help for the poor victims. It takes three to four years before the Catholic Church will even take notice of them."

Father Rookey explained that in order to propagate his healing ministry, he must spend several hours a day in prayer, and indicated that he fasts a lot on bread and water. Although he is not an officially designated Exorcist, he was well prepared for this unscheduled one by virtue of his healing ministry. He also explained that canon lawyers agreed with him that "love" dictated not to just leave the man there suffering. Thus, his reason for carrying out the exorcism as he did.

Frankie indeed attended the Healing Mass the following evening at Saint Vincent Palloti Catholic Church in Hadderfield, New Jersey. Father Rookey, a devout and very holy man with a sense of humor, again opened the service with a couple of one-liners that he got from his good friend, Bob Hope, like: "Where's the one place a person can go and get the warmest reception of anywhere else? Why it's hell, of course." And, "I've been a priest for over fifty years and they still call me 'that Rookey priest.'"

Frankie came up to the altar again at Saint Vincent Pallotti Church, surrounded by his entire family, and received the special blessing from Father Rookey, and again he "rested in the Spirit." But this time he came out of it with no problem and no demons. He was cheered by the five hundred fifty participants when he got up to witness and tell his story of being "possessed" from the night before in Doylestown. Frankie had "beat the devil" and apparently now had been healed. Evidently, the demon in question was sent back to receive a "warm reception."

Don Meehan

It was not just a question of mind over matter for Scottish born Heather Duncan whose crushed spine was apparently healed in a "laying on of hands" last year by Father Peter Rookey. She, for one, believes in miracles.

Heather, a non-practicing believer, who was nursing at the Geriatric Unit in the Glenburn Wing of Woodend General Hospital in Aberdeen, suffered from an accident in 1985 which left her spinal cord damaged and nerves crushed. Until last October, she could not even make a cup of tea. She relied on the patience of her husband and home-help to live.

Heather, during her visit to Ireland as a witness to Father Rookey's healing, recalls her trauma and the overwhelming experience of once again being able to walk although medically she should be unable to. Forced to live in a wheelchair supported by braces to keep her sitting upright, Heather said: "I genuinely believed from that point onwards that my mission was to suffer and that I should offer it up. I wanted to go on a pilgrimage of thanksgiving."

It was in a little graveyard in Medjugorje, where thousands of pilgrims flock each year to pay tribute to Our Lady, that she met Father Rookey. He asked me what was wrong, and I told him I couldn't walk. He asked me to hold the Crucifix and to look at the face of Jesus. He laid his hands on my head and on my shoulders, down my legs and arms and all the time was praying quietly. He gave me a prayer and then I remember nothing except intense burning and heat especially where he was touching my back. Then I felt dizzy and had I not been in a wheelchair would have fallen for sure.

Witnesses of the event described to Heather how she looked as if she was unconscious, with her body shaking violently and trembling. Father Rookey asked if she believed that Jesus could heal her, to which she replied "Yes."

Heather said: "He asked me did I want to try and stand up and he took me by the tips of the fingers and I spontaneously began to walk backwards and forwards."

Since then, Heather has been medically examined by a series of doctors. Medically her spine is still crushed, yet she walks. A television documentary has been made about her and other "miraculous" healings. Before it was recorded, doctors were called in to examine her spine. Their findings were the same.

Heather, now is a lively active young woman. She accompanied Father Rookey on his visit to Ireland to assist him as a witness to her story. What is striking is her intense level of faith. She accepts without cynicism or question her "miracle." Others she leaves to doubt.

Heather Duncan

In 1980, I was diagnosed with Rheumatoid Arthritis. I feel confident that many of you reading this will be able to relate to the pain and misery that arthritis can cause. The first five years of my illness was very difficult. It was an effort for me to button my shirt, and, in order to start my car, I had to use both hands to turn the ignition key. Many simple tasks were monumental for me. In order to maintain a fair standard of life because of this illness, I would, on six week intervals, receive cortisone injections in my hands and my knees. I would also have to have fluid removed from my knees.

On August 15, 1994, the Feast of the Assumption, I attended a healing service conducted by Father Peter Mary Rookey, O.S.M., at Immaculate Conception Church in Marrero, Louisiana. As I was approaching the altar, I was placed to the extreme right of it. For some reason, I was asked to move to the center of the altar where the Blessed Sacrament was exposed. As I waited for Father to come and give me his blessing, I looked up at the Blessed Sacrament, and I asked Jesus to grant me His peace and love. I did not ask for a healing. Father came, blessed me, and I rested in the Spirit. Shortly after I went to bed that night, I felt this heat come over my body. My initial reaction was that I was experiencing a "flare up" which happens, at times, to people suffering with Rheumatoid Arthritis. I realized this heat was not the same as the type that comes from a "flare up." It made me restless, and I could not go to sleep while this sensation was occurring.

A few days passed, and I put it out of my mind. On September 7, 1994, the opening day of the Novena to Our Lady of Sorrows, I had a doctor's appointment. As usual, he examined my hands and knees. To his surprise, I had no inflammation in my hands or in my knees. Since there was no inflammation or fluid present, I did not need a cortisone shot. I related the story of the healing service to my doctor, but all he did was look at me kind of funny. His only response to me was that he had watched a few healing services on television. I requested a blood test in order to document my diagnosis of Rheumatoid Arthritis. On September 11, I received a call from my doctor's office advising me that the results of the blood test were negative. I had no Rheumatoid factor in my blood. I could not believe this happened. I was truly healed of this illness. To confirm this healing, it is documented on

David Parkes

my medical records that I had blood work done in 1992, and the results were positive for Rheumatoid Arthritis.

I wish to take this opportunity to publicly thank Jesus for this healing, and I would also like to honor His Blessed Mother for all the wonderful graces received through her intercession. I thank God for sending Father Rookey to us.

Elson Legendre, S.O.S.M.

My name is David Parkes, and I stared death in the face. Four years ago, I became the victim of severe Chrons Disease. I had undergone ten major bowel operations with the last one taking eleven hours. The medical specialists who took care of me offered no hope. Before my illness, I was five feet, eleven inches and weighed two-hundred thirty pounds. By the time this illness ran its course, I was down to one-hundred ten pounds. I had no idea Chrons Disease, which affects the bowel, was such a debilitating illness. I lived with a constant, intense pain in my stomach with no food or drink being able to stay down.

At one time, I was a professional soccer player who gave up sports to concentrate on a career in music. By the end of 1977, I had the world at my feet. I won a prestigious national talent contest in Ireland, and I became a band leader as well as a singer. From winning the contest, I was invited to perform in a variety show with a contract for twelve weeks. My doctors were not happy with me because I would not enter the hospital for treatment until the show was over. ' We compromised by my going to the hospital as an outpatient. However, I collapsed after eight weeks, and the major operations began. Because of complications, I had three more surgeries in the next four years. I was told I was a singing success, but all I did was survive from performance to performance, from surgery to surgery.

When I became ill, Anne, my wife, and I had been married for five years with two small children. Lorna was two when Ken was born. At birth, Ken was diagnosed with Cystic Fibrosis. I was very bitter about this, and my bitterness grew worse with my diagnosis of Chrons Disease. Because of Father Gus and the talk he gave me, I was able to go on with my life. I told God I had to get well because Ken had to be able to live a full life. Anne and I had another son, Gary, who was born perfectly healthy.

In January, 1989, I had the tenth surgery, and I was told there was nothing else that could be done for me. I was devastated. I feared, not only a hopeless future, but severe financial problems. My friends organized a benefit night for me where I sang briefly at what those present believed to be my last performance.

Life has many twists and turns. At the benefit, there were two people present, who, unbeknownst to me, would play a significant part in my life. These two people owned a travel agency, and they were involved in organizing pilgrimages to Medjugorje. Heather Parsons, one of the owners of the travel agency, is also the author of "A Light Between The Hills." Later, she told me that as soon as she looked at me she thought, "If that is David Parkes, and I send him to Medjugorje with Father Peter Mary Rookey, he'll be totally healed." The following day an invitation was issued by Heather's business partner to Anne and myself to take one of their pilgrimages with an American healing priest by the name of Father Peter Mary Rookey, O.S.M., from Chicago. I really did not want to go.

Not only did I have a problem with religion throughout my fourteen year illness, I also had a problem in my marriage. We had separated twice during my long medical ordeal. Anne knew how I felt about the Church, but she remembered something that happened during one of my stays in the hospital. She heard me whisper, "Oh God, how I'd love to go back to Yugoslavia." We spent our honeymoon there in a little fishing village, Cavtat, eight kilometers from the coast of Dubrovnik. Anne reminded me of the sunshine and warmth of the village, as well as my desire to return with a camera to capture the beauty of the city of Dubrovnik. I gave in, and accepted the invitation.

Even though I gave up on my faith, Anne never gave up on hers. She turned even more to her faith to give her the strength she needed at this time. Anne had a great devotion to Our Lord and Our Lady. Feeling very threatened by her faith, I sat her down before we left for the airport to tell her I did not want to hear about religion nor did I want to hear any prayers in my presence while we were on this trip. She reluctantly agreed.

After checking in at the Dublin Airport, we went to the departure gate where we were introduced to our spiritual director, Father Rookey. When I shook hands with him, I felt threatened by the outpouring of love and compassion that came my way. We talked for a few minutes, and then, we went our separate ways. Once we arrived in Dubrovnik, we were assigned to our buses for the three hour trip to Medjugorje.

My trouble started during the last twenty minutes of our bus ride. A lovely young lady, our courier, got up in front of the bus and started to say the Rosary. I went berserk. I reminded Anne of our agreement while shouting I wanted to get off the bus. The courier continued praying, and the bus continued to Medjugorje without stopping. During the remainder of the trip, I was in a complete state of agitation.

When we arrived, I could not wait to get to the hotel. I was surprised when all I saw was a one story building with two big wings sticking up the middle. As I walked closer, I realized the two wings were a stairwell. We unpacked, changed into comfortable clothing, and went to look at this place called Medjugorje. We passed a few houses, a couple of businesses, and an enormous church. "Is this it?" I asked. "Tomorrow morning we are going to Dubrovnik."

The following morning Anne was up early with a different idea. She woke me up early and told me, out of respect to Father, we had to attend his Mass and healing service. I agreed but told her we were leaving right after the services for Dubrovnik. Mass lasted one and a half hours, and Father Peter was not even on the altar. After Mass, we went to the vineyard behind the church for the healing service.

It took me a long time to arrive at the healing service, because I walked so slowly. The physical pain I felt was awful. I was gaunt, bent over, and could not stand up straight due to the pain I experienced. Once we arrived, we saw three Irish priests with Father Peter. Hundreds of people formed a semi-circle around them on a paved area. I watched as Father placed his hands on people's heads, and then I would watch them fall down to the ground. I told Anne it was mass hysteria, and that the people were faking it. Once one did it, they all did it.

I left Anne there, and told her I was going to take pictures of the mountainside. When I returned, it looked like a battlefield with all the bodies strewn everywhere. I had to walk over them to get to Anne. She asked me if I wanted to be blessed. I told her "No," and went off to take more photographs. I returned only to hear Anne again ask me to receive a blessing. I did so just to keep her quiet.

Three priests blessed me before Father Rookey came up to me putting his Crucifix into my hand. Father asked me if there was anything I wanted to tell him. I told him I had two major surgeries in the last couple of months, and that I was in a great deal of pain. I told him the doctors told me I was very sick, and that it was only a matter of time before I would die. Father dipped his thumb into the Holy Oil, blessed my forehead, and put his hands on my head while praying. Before I rested in the Spirit, I remember Father taking the Crucifix from my hand. As I opened my eyes, I was convinced someone had hit me. I stood up, dusted myself off rather sheepishly, and asked what happened. I was told the Spirit was with me very strongly because I had been out for twenty minutes.

I remember lying on the ground and being aware of the people singing around me. When I stood up, I was experiencing an intense burning inside my body which went from the tips of my toes to the top of my head. I did not realize I had been healed.

A day and a half had gone by before I realized I was completely out of pain. I was able to eat, stand up straight, and I even had color in my cheeks. All the weakness I had previously felt was also gone. Anne knew me well enough to know I would not fake anything. It was while we were climbing up Podbrdo that Anne suggested to me that God had healed me.

As we turned the bend on the top of Podbrdo, I felt a great peace descend upon me. I tried to pray but I could not. All I could say was, "Lord, teach me to pray." After a while, Anne and I embraced. I had found inner peace, and now I was able to make peace with my wife. I realized, at this point, if God sent me down my cross to carry again, and He gave me the choice of the physical or spiritual healing, I would take the spiritual one. When I went home and kept my doctor's appointment, he stood in astonishment. He told me to keep doing whatever it was I was doing.

David Parkes

I had never heard of Father Rookey until last June when my feet guided me into a bookstore in Killarney, Ireland. Because I teach seventh and eight grade Religion classes at Immaculate Conception School in Chicago, the title, **Man of Miracles**, grabbed my attention. My students desperately need and want any information which helps them hang onto their beliefs.

I read the book on the plane going home, and I remembered wishing that I could meet Father Rookey. I also recall thinking that I'd ask for a blessing to heal my spine. The pain was bothering me even seated on the plane. I had suffered from Osteo-Arthritis for eighteen years.

Last November, someone told me that a certain Father Rookey would be present for Mass at the home of Jim and Eileen Staunton. I was given the address, and left home that

Monday night with the book tucked under my arms. I was hoping Father might autograph it.

The prayer session began at 7:00 P.M., and at 9:00 P.M., Father came out into our midst to begin Mass. My back was "singing in pain" to me by this time. I was truly tempted to leave, but could not gracefully do so without disrupting the peace of the crowded living room. When Mass ended, everyone began folding their chairs and storing them in the hallway. I thought, "Here's my chance. I'm out of here!"

I tiptoed down to the family room, and put on my coat. As I reached the top of the stairs, a woman asked where I was going. I told her I was tired and was going home because it was getting late. By this time, it was 9:45 P.M. The woman said to go in and watch the healing service. I asked who was being healed, and at that time, I felt a gentle nudge. I can only assume this nudge came from my angel who was guiding me to the front row with gentle hands. Father was before me in a flash. I recall hearing his words, "Surrender to the Spirit."

Down I went! What a feeling of love, peace and joy! I rested in the Spirit for some time, and when I moved to get up off the floor, I was amazed that all the pain I had been experiencing was gone!

I said nothing to anyone until I went home. When I arrived home, I told my very skeptical husband. He read Father Rookey's book the next day, and went to the next prayer meeting when Father was present. He also, "rested in the Spirit," and has had a conversion of faith since then.

Praise Jesus! Thank You Jesus, Mary and Father Rookey! Bless you Margaret, for helping spread the word.

Mary Kay Galvin

It is more than ten years since my husband and I first met Father Peter Mary Rookey. He came to the Mary Immaculate Queen Center in Lombard, Illinois to say Mass for the Messengers, and later, he assisted Father Kelligher at Saint Pius Church, which is also in Lombard, with his healing service.

We have known the Servites since the early 1950s when they had the Sorrowful Mother Novena at the Basilica of Our Lady of Sorrows in Chicago. We have attended many healing Masses in Ireland, as well as throughout the United States, with Father Rookey. During his service, he always tells his congregation that he is only the instrument. Jesus is the healer, and he gives all glory to Jesus.

Seven years ago, we started a prayer meeting which is held in our home. We invited Father to come, and say Mass for our group as well as conduct a healing service. Now, we are blessed to have him every Monday night when he is available. Many members of our prayer group have been touched with the feelings of love, joy and peace. We all hope and pray that God will leave him with us for many years to come. At our Monday night service, we have many sick and invalid people who come to pray and to be blessed, because they are unable to travel to the various churches where Father has his services.

Margaret, we thank you for the great work you are doing. May God bless you in all your endeavors.

Jim and Eileen Staunton

In the spring of 1992, medical tests showed a growth on my thyroid. At the time, my doctors showed no concern; however, problems began occurring during the summer of the same year. I began having difficulty breathing, and was constantly tired. I kept going, but was losing weight. By the beginning of July, I lost nearly ten pounds, and was having gynecological problems.

Suddenly, I wasn't able to walk. I was able to get to Church and my prayer group, but my steps became slower and smaller until I could only inch forward. It was as if both legs were tied together. My skull and neck felt as if they were on fire. With the weight loss becoming worse, I decided it was time to return to a doctor.

Upon hearing I had a growth on my thyroid, the doctor immediately referred me to an endocrinologist at Loyola University in Maywood. A battery of tests were done, and all results were normal. I had been unaware that the cyst on my thyroid was filled with fluid which was blocking my air passage, I was strongly advised to have it aspirated.

On Monday, August 15, 1994, the Feast of Our Lady's Assumption, the aspiration was done with no anesthetic. I was told the cyst could return, but I pray to God that it doesn't. When the results came back from the lab, it was determined that the cyst was benign. I was finally able to breathe and swallow again, but I could not get my legs to walk.

I attended my prayer group and Father Rookey was there to celebrate Mass. Because I wasn't able to walk, Communion was brought to me. At the end of Mass, Father prayed over me and many others. Leaving the prayer group, I wasn't able to walk normally, but I declined the use of a wheelchair when I was offered it. I persevered while inching toward the car.

I had the chance to attend Mass on Monday, August 22, 1994. Dad drove Mom and I along with our neighbor to 5:00 P.M. Mass at Immaculate Conception Church in Chicago. When I entered the church, I knew I wanted to be as close to the Tabernacle as possible. I began praying fervently as I pulled myself from pew to pew. My fervency increased as Mass built up to the Consecration which is the most powerful part of the Mass. My prayer was simple. I said, "Lord, if You will it, I can walk out of Church. Only You can heal me." At the same time, I thanked Jesus.

During the Consecration, the pain left. When it came time to receive Holy Communion, I made my way slowly to the priest. He knew me, and leaning over, he said to me, "You're not feeling well, are you?" I said I wasn't, and I needed his prayers. As soon as the priest gave me Jesus, I began walking back to my pew. Both my mom and my neighbor saw this and were astounded.

Mom left when Mass was over to make sure Dad was outside. I told my neighbor I was healed, and we both hugged each other and cried. I walked out of Church as though there had never been a problem. After getting out of the car in the garage, I told Mom what had happened, and to prove it, raced her to the back door. I told her I was healed after receiving Holy Communion and she was speechless. She and our neighbor saw me walk because I had received Holy Communion first. I've been walking everywhere without pain, and have had no more problems which require the services of a gynecologist. JESUS IS PRESENT IN THE HOLY EUCHARIST. He is all loving and powerful. If only people would realize this and believe.

At the time I was healed, the gift of tears was given to me. Each time I receive Holy Communion, tears well up in my eyes and roll down my cheeks. I believe it is a closer relationship to Jesus. Prior to my healing, I would always pray to Jesus after Communion, but I never shed tears. On September 1, 1994, I returned to my doctor for a follow up exam. It was discovered at this time my weight had returned to exactly what it was before I became ill.

I've been sharing my healing experience in any way I can. I share by letter, phone, face-to-face, and in front of the Staunton prayer group, "Mother of Christ," as well as the congregation at St. Francis Borgia. The Monday before I was healed, Father Peter Rookey anointed me and prayed over me. He also brought Holy Communion to me in my chair because I was unable to walk. When I witnessed at St. Francis Borgia, he was delighted to see me walking.

Jesus is the Divine Physician Who heals if it is His Will. I am waiting for the Lord to remove the spasms I am experiencing so I can seek His Will.

Irene Hand

Even though people would tell me I had a lot of faith, I never considered myself to be a person who did have a great deal of faith. I always believed that anyone who saw Mary or Christ was a saint. At one time if anyone would have told me that God spoke to them, I would have considered them crazy. I guess I am like Saint Thomas, because a part of me would have to have proof in order to believe.

God is merciful, and He is always eager to help us grow closer to Him. I grew up believing that God did not love me. However, He showed me His love for me as well as His love for all His children.

My wife, Madeline, told me about a healing priest, Father Peter Rookey. By the way she talked about him, I knew I had to receive whatever I could from him. I attended his healing Mass, and I had him pray over me. In my eagerness to be a part of this beautiful service, I volunteered to be a catcher for those who "rest in the Spirit." One of the people that Father Rookey was praying over was a gentlemen in a wheelchair. We were asked to place our hands toward the person in the wheelchair. We were also asked to pray. While I was praying, I felt an immense surge of power flow from me through my hands toward the gentleman. It was such a great joy being able to be used by the Lord. It never ceases to amaze me how the Lord touches my doubting heart by witnessing His healing power through the people who are healed.

> Your brother and servant in Christ,
> Daryle

Father Peter Rookey is a man with a twinkle in both eyes, and a touch of Irish laughter. He is small in stature but big in heart. Father is no ordinary priest as his ministry has been linked to many miracles. I was eager to meet him, and my opportunity came in Wichita, Kansas several years ago at a Marian Conference where the "Rookey Priest" was the featured speaker to the thousands of the faithful.

Father followed Father Ken Roberts, and things proceeded calmly enough until he called the priests to assist him in blessing the people. Father Rookey first anointed the priests with Holy Oil, and they fell back hitting the floor like nine pins. I was one of those priests, and have kept in communication with this man ever since our first meeting. Occasionally, I am blessed with being able to assist him at his monthly Mass at Mary, Queen of the Universe Church in Saint Louis.

I am always inspired by Father. Even though he is 79 years old, he continues to maintain a most demanding schedule. People everywhere, especially in England and Ireland, look forward to being blessed by him. Indeed, the people of Ireland welcome him as one of their own, and he is in danger of becoming an honorary leprechaun. May God continue to bless this Servite priest and son of Mary who works and prays with great effect to bring into focus the healing ministry of Jesus to the people of God.

On a more spiritual note, Father Rookey has inspired me to seek healing for myself, and also to pray for the healing of others. This inspiration has brought a sense of deeper fulfillment in the priesthood as well as a deep conviction that a healing ministry is at the heart of the Church.

Father Bill Keogh

My name is Father Bill Keogh, and I am a Catholic Chaplain at the Jefferson City Correctional Center in St. Louis, Missouri. I am also the Pastor of a small, rural church in Folk, Missouri.

Father Bill Keogh

My name is Juanita Brown, and I have cancer. Approximately two years ago, I was diagnosed with breast cancer. My doctor immediately removed my right breast with chemotherapy treatments following for many months. Upon completion of the treatments, I, as well as my doctors, assumed I was cured.

I started having problems with my right ear, and this past September had to have surgery on it to correct the problem. After the surgery, I never regained my strength, and it was discovered by my doctor that the cancer had resurfaced to four spots on my spine. My heart was heavy with sadness because I knew my life expectancy was short.

My body gradually began to deteriorate. I lost over fifty pounds, and I became bed ridden. My body was racked with pain, and the only time I left my house was to go to and from the doctor's office. As time went on, I had to use a wheelchair, because I did not have the strength to walk. The pain was excruciating. My days consisted of staying in bed heavily sedated with medication that did not ease the pain. I was sure I was not going to live much longer. I prayed, cried, and prayed some more.

On December 22, my life took an "about face." My friend, Gene and her son, Jonathan, spent the day with me which was also her birthday. She kept telling me not to give up, because God was going to see me through this crisis. Gene told me I was traveling down the road God had prepared for me, and that I had come across a mountain I had to climb. She told me this mountain was only a small obstacle, and she had faith I would overcome it. Gene told me I was put on earth for a purpose, and I had yet to fulfill that purpose.

Later, we were in my bedroom going through my mail. I could no longer do the simplest of tasks. Gene was sitting on the floor on the side of my bed when she picked up the December issue of Mary's Helpers newsletter. As she picked it up, something went flying through the air. I asked her quietly what was flying in the air. She told me it was a prayer card, and handed it to me. The prayer turned out to be the **Miracle Prayer** on one side and a photo of Father Peter Mary Rookey on the reverse side. I immediately started saying it. It was then I decided that God was not going to give up on me, and I was going to live. The prayer was my sign from God.

I called my doctor the following week, and informed him I wanted a second opinion on my illness. My request was granted, and the week after Christmas I started seeing another oncologist, I had to travel a greater distance to get to my new doctor's office, but I did not mind. With God's help, I began to feel spiritually uplifted. I am now going into the third phase of my cancer treatment, and with each new day, I feel I am getting stronger. I now know God has a purpose in life for me. If it had not been for that special prayer, I am sure I would not have survived the New Year. My prayers were answered. I know the **Miracle Prayer** was the sign I had been waiting for. It strengthened my faith, and gave me the courage, as well as the determination, to fight my dreaded disease. I have my life, my faith, my family, and most of all my loving friends who refused to let me give up. I wish to give a special "thank you" to Gene who had been by my side since the very first sign of my cancer. Thank You, God, for everything.

Juanita Brown

Father Peter Rookey is the brother of my dad, Robert Rookey. He has had a big influence on my life since I was very young. I am forty-three years old, and I am one of the few people attending my uncle's services who can say he has known Father Peter for over forty years. He has been remembered in my daily prayers ever since I learned to pray. When he would return from Europe, he would come to Superior, Wisconsin to visit our family. I would run into his arms, and he would take my hands and whirl me around and around until I got dizzy.

He sometimes ate supper at my family's house, and he always had a barrel of good jokes to tell us that would make all the family laugh as heartily as we ate. When I was a teenager and in my twenties, he and I would go for long walks around Superior. It was at this time that we would have good talks about God and other aspects of life. He really impressed me a lot, one dark evening when, just before saying good-by, he reminded me that "the more you think of yourself, the smaller you are and the less you think of yourself, the bigger you are." These few words taught me to put others first if I intended to do God's Will.

In eighth grade, I sang in the Superior Cathedral Church of Christ the King choir for the 25th Jubilee Mass honoring Father Peter for a quarter century of priestly service.

125

Timothy Rookey & Bernard Rookey

In May 1991, I also attended his Golden Jubilee Mass at Our Lady of Sorrows Basilica in Chicago.

In 1991, Father Peter was very instrumental in the revival of my Catholic faith when I first attended one of his healing services in Milwaukee, and then accompanied him in May of that same year to Medjugorje. He heard my first confession in many years, and he taught me to pray the Rosary once again. I praise the good Lord and Our Blessed Mother for my conversion through the power of my loving uncle, Father Peter.

I returned with him to Medjugorje in May 1993, and I brought a young lady with me who was a recent convert to Catholicism. That same young woman, Anne Elizabeth Becker, is now my beautiful wife. Good things happen when you hang around Father Peter, let me tell you! When he calls, God picks up on the first ring!

I keep in touch with Father Peter by telephone and by meeting with him after his First Saturday services at Our Lady of Sorrows Basilica. Last weekend, May 6, 1995, my wife, Anne, our good friend, Evan Stremenski, who is a Croatian-American, and I attended his service. We met with him later for coffee and pastry at his priory home in the Chicago suburbs. He seldom occupies it as he spends so much time conducting healing services all around this country and the world. During his homily on May 6, he announced that the Lord had been putting it on him for some time to grow a beard. He said he never had worn one before and disliked the feel of it. However, he emphatically said he was going to wear a beard until ABORTION is ABORTED!!!

I love my uncle, Father Peter, and love God and Our Mother Mary for blessing me with him all of my life.

Timothy Peter Rookey

On July 14, 1994, my father-in-law suffered a severe stroke. The night before the stroke he attended his 49ers' supper and was feeling fine at the time. When he returned home, he watched a little television and went to bed. During the night, he woke up not feeling very well. He stayed up for a while but decided to go back to bed.

Around 6:00 A.M., he got up, and he and my mother-in-law started to make coffee. When he poured his cup, he spilled it. My mother-in-law could see that something was wrong. She started asking him about his supper the night before, but he could not tell her. She called their children. When they arrived, he was not able to talk nor use his right side.

We called 911 for assistance. When he left for West Jefferson Hospital, he was able to say a few words as well as lift his right arm and leg a little. In the Emergency Room, he seemed to be getting worse. After he was admitted, the doctor told us that he had suffered a severe stroke which was caused by total blockage of the left carotid artery. As the days went by, he was becoming very depressed. We had to put a no-visitors sign on his door because, when his friends came by to see him, he was unable to communicate with them. He stayed in West Jefferson Hospital for one week. On July 20, 1994, he was transferred to the Rehab Center of New Orleans. His progress was very slow, and again he was very depressed. He remained at the Rehab Center as an in-patient until August 16, 1994, after which he started as an out-patient, and is still attending three days a week.

On September 7, 1994, the Novena to Our Lady of Sorrows began with Father Rookey. We brought him to the healing service on Thursday, September 8, 1994. Father Rookey prayed on him. After he was prayed on by Father, he was able to stand on his own, and he pushed me out of the

Tony Brown

Church in his wheelchair. At this time, he walks with a cane and he speaks well. His right arm is slowly progressing. Now, he wants to have the independence he once had. After the service, I asked him what he felt. He said, "Strength, peace and happiness." The doctors are amazed by his progress, and they say he is doing "GREAT!"

I would like to praise God and thank Father Rookey and Mary's Helpers for such a beautiful Novena.

Diane Orgeron

I first met Father Rookey in 1993 when Margaret Trosclair brought him to WTIX radio for the Mary's Helpers News Program. He was a most likable individual who possessed a sense of humor, as well as a warmth, that generated good feelings among those in his midst.

Being in the presence of Father has lifted any doubts about the existence of God in my mind. It has been said many times that he has the power to heal through Christ. Even though I had heard him recite the **Healing Prayer** on Mary's Helpers News Program, I was about to see him in action. Because of a very generous individual, I was able to be a part of the twenty-four pilgrims who traveled to Medjugorje from New Orleans to celebrate the 13th Anniversary of the first apparition. Father was our spiritual director during this pilgrimage.

On June 24, 1994, we were on Apparition Hill when Father rose from the spot where he had been meditating and walked over to where a young man from France was lying on a stretcher unable to walk. Father asked him if he wanted him to pray for him. The young man said yes, and Father Rookey began the prayer. People crowded around as Father continued to pray over the young Frenchman. Father asked the young man if he would like to try to get up.

At first, the young man was unable to do so. At that point, I noticed Father Rookey was reaching into his breast pocket. From his pocket, he took out his Servite Crucifix. He began praying over the French fellow more intensely. A swell of people began to crowd around, and I was pushed further away from Father. Because of my location, I was unable to hear Father ask the young man to rise, but I could see him reach out his hand. As the young man began to get up, the shouts of praises to God, as well as the Hail Mary, could be heard everywhere. This Frenchman, who just one hour before had to be carried up Apparition Hill on a stretcher by his four friends, stood up, bent over and touched his toes. He also raised his arms above his head and began to walk around.

Father Rookey, through prayer, faith and Jesus Christ, had performed a miracle on the site of the first apparition on Apparition Hill. I had been blessed by God, Jesus, Mary, and my sponsor. Because of this very generous person, I was able to witness with my own eyes this miracle. For had I not known the circumstances around the event, I would have doubted it.

The people on Apparition Hill began to cheer, cry and sing the "Ave Maria." They began to surge in on Father Rookey, and it was at this time that I remember thinking how drained he appeared after this healing. It seemed to me that people were coming out of nowhere asking Father to heal this one and that one. It reminded me of one of the Biblical stories of Christ being overwhelmed by people wanting Him to heal them.

Tony Brown

Gayle Ponseti
Mary's Helpers Secretary

My name is Gayle Ponseti. I am the staff secretary of Mary's Helpers, Inc. which is a non-profit organization founded by Margaret Trosclair on February 1, 1987. Mary's Helpers was founded to help spread the messages of the Blessed Virgin Mary all over the country and the world. I have been working with Margaret for nearly eight years, and I was present when Father Peter Mary Rookey, O.S.M., first became involved with Mary's Helpers. What first amazed me about Father was the fact that he knew he was coming to New Orleans to be a part of the enshrinement celebration for the replica statue of Our Lady of Lourdes of Medjugorje on the Feast of Our Lady of the Holy Rosary, October 7, 1988, before we ever asked him.

When the celebration was in the planning stages, Margaret and I had a discussion concerning the selection of a guest speaker. The festivities were to include a two mile candlelight rosary procession. She talked to me about a healing priest, Father Rookey, whom she met briefly following a healing service held by him in the cemetery in Medjugorje on one of her earlier pilgrimages. Cathy McCarthy, who was on that pilgrimage, had suggested him to Margaret when she heard of Margaret's need for a guest speaker. Margaret brought this suggestion to her pastor, Father Richard Maughan, whose church, Visitation of Our Lady, would house the statue. Father Maughan did not feel comfortable with the "healing priest," so Margaret never pursued it any further. Not once did we contact Father Rookey or his office.

In our efforts to acquire a guest speaker, Margaret and I contacted celebrities like Mother Angelica, Mother Teresa, Bob Hope, and Loretta Young. Meanwhile, different people who knew about Mary's Helpers were running into Father Rookey in Medjugorje during his many pilgrimages there. In conversations with him, their point of origin usually came up.

He said, "I'm going to New Orleans in October." Their answer was the usual, "Really?" Upon returning home, they called us to ask if we knew anything about it, and we told them we didn't. Margaret and I looked at each other with a question on our faces. We definitely knew we had not made any contact with him whatsoever. "Maybe someone else in the area had invited him for their function," we thought. When this happened the second time, the name "Mary's Helpers" was part of Father Rookey's statement. Margaret and I thought, "If neither of us invited him, who did?" When this happened the third time, I told Margaret that she needed to contact this priest who thinks he's coming to let him know he's not, no matter who invited him.

After exhausting all other avenues here, for having a celebrity guest and with time running out, Margaret planned to approach Father Maughan again telling him of her failure. She hoped that he might change his mind since Father Rookey thought he was coming anyway.

It just so happened that Father Maughan had received bad news concerning his mother who lived in Ireland. She had been in an accident, and he needed to rush home. Margaret knew she had to get him before he left because she did not know how long he would be gone. She got a chance to talk to him as he was on his way out. She told him that she had tried everybody whom they talked about, but none were available. Then she said, "How about the healing priest?" And he said, "Okay, Margaret." Now Margaret had Father's permission, and she was free to contact Father Rookey for the first time.

This was the first of many encounters I have had with Father Peter Mary Rookey, O.S.M. I was personally involved with this one, and it has left a lasting impression on me. Every time I have been in Father's company, whether it is on a pilgrimage or just sitting talking, I have always been struck by

131

his continuous prayer life. His fingers are always on his Rosary. Sometimes it is the five decade chaplet and sometimes it is the Seven Dolor Rosary. Many times he dozes off only to wake up and continue to pray his Rosary. He always has a Hail Mary on his lips.

Five years later, April 1993, I was privileged to be the coordinator for Mary's Helpers pilgrimage to Rome and the Shrines of Italy with Father Rookey. One of the draws for this pilgrimage was to be in Saint Peter's Square for the Beatification of Sister Faustina on Divine Mercy Sunday. Four other "saints to be" were honored the same day, two others from Poland, one from Spain and, one from Italy. Sister Faustina was the most highly honored one, because the painting of her was the largest and it hung from the balcony of the Basilica in the middle of the others. There must have been two million people in the Square which consisted of: all of Poland, half of Spain, and Italy, who were already there. Many, many Americans came because of the "Marian Helpers" movement to spread the Divine Mercy devotion in the United States and Canada, as well as other countries from around the world. We stood for three hours in the hot sun because we were unable to get seats, except if we brought our own. It was during this time that I realized how well-known Father Rookey had become. Fifteen minutes did not go by without someone from another part of the world stopping to say "Hello" to him. People from China, Japan, Australia, New Zealand, England, Ireland, and other countries all stopped to speak to him. The next day, during the audience with the Holy Father, we were able to get seats, but it was the same thing all over again with Father Rookey.

During our stay in Rome, Father took Margaret and me walking all over the city when we had free time. Our hotel was just two blocks from the Vatican, and each time we went out, we walked through Saint Peter's Square with Father

Rookey as our tour guide. Father lived there for many years and really knows his way around. The Servants of Mary (Servites), Father Rookey's Order, have a motherhouse in Rome, San Marcello on the Corso, which is near the Forum.

On each of our walks to visit San Marcello or just to see Rome with Father, we got a good look at the Roman architecture which is breath-taking. One can only stand in awe of the masters who built them. I found the outside of some buildings dreary and in the need of a good cleaning; however, when I walked by an open doorway, I saw a complete contrast. The insides were well kept, clean and beautiful. On another evening walk, Father brought us to see the Fountain of Treve. This seemed to be a favorite hang out for the young people because there were many there. We visited San Marcello several times as well as other Church parishes staffed by Servites including one that has a miraculous well. Father liked bringing us to the Servite churches and houses because we had been working to get the Secular Servites started in the New Orleans area. Margaret and I had been drawn to Our Lady of Sorrows, but it was through Father Rookey that we felt a calling to become Servites.

Father Rookey likes to walk. In fact, he likes to walk at a clip (fast). Both Margaret and I found it hard keeping up with him. If that wasn't bad enough, he also likes to run up stairs skipping every other step, and there are plenty of steps in Rome. "Where DOES he find the strength and the energy?" A man twenty years older than me! My goodness!

We always returned to our hotel late at night, and it was always too late to purchase a bus ticket. The only place they could be purchased was at news stands, and they closed at 7:00 P.M. Father did not like to take taxis because he thought their rates were too high. So, we would end up walking all the way back. Margaret and I looked at each other a lot, but we went right along with it laughing as we walked. We weren't unhappy about the first or second time, but we just did not have his stamina. We were running out of gas, and Rome was the first stop on the pilgrimage. It didn't help that I had on my good walking shoes.

On our last night in Rome, we were invited to dine with his brother friars at San Marcello. Near the end of dinner, I leaned over to Margaret and whispered, "You and Father Rookey can walk back if you want to, but Gayle Ponseti is going to ride back, somehow, even in a taxi." Father Rookey's brother friars either know him very well and how much he likes to walk, or they over heard me whisper "Oh No!" when he said "we'll walk back because it was not so far" every night and they felt sorry for us. When we were ready to leave, they handed Father Rookey something he could not refuse, bus tickets. BUS TICKETS! The Lord had mercy on us.

I told everyone, upon my return home, that I could not get lost in Rome if I were blindfolded. I could GIVE tours of Rome. Father Rookey walked us everywhere.

Just remember, if you are going with Father Rookey, expect to walk. Ha, Ha! Ha, Ha! Ha, Ha! And I'm still laughing.

I love you, Father Rookey.

Gayle Ponseti, S.O.S.M.

A miracle happened at the healing service in Medjugorje on Sunday, June 25, 1995. When Father Rookey placed his hands on my forehead, I asked for a healing for my husband. I asked Jesus to fill him with His love and also love from Mary. Even though we have been hurting with a difficult marriage for thirty-nine years, we have been blessed with five children and five grandchildren.

I was resting in the Spirit and when I woke up I could not stop crying. I was crying uncontrollably. This was the first time in my life I ever cried like this. I knew that Jesus and Mary, through Father Rookey, was healing us as well as working a miracle. I had a vision of the Sacred Heart of Jesus and the Immaculate Heart of Mary saying, "We will take care of you and your husband. Surrender this totally to Us. Believe and know that We love your husband and We will fill him with Our Love. Do not be concerned about your lack of love for him anymore."

Flo

Father Peter Mary Rookey, O.S.M.
Circa 1996

On June 19, 1995, Father Rookey, Gayle Ponseti and I brought a group of pilgrims to Medjugorje for the 14th Anniversary. When Father met us at the airport in New York, he met us with a new look. We were shocked when we saw him with a beard. In fact, he didn't look like Father Rookey at all. He was totally different. I was surprised because I was not aware he had grown one. Finally, when I was able to look at him, I realized how youthful he looked. He was a little slimmer and not as tired looking. His movements and actions were of a different person. He was so energetic we could not keep up with him going up either mountain. Each day, after the English Mass in Medjugorje, Father conducted a healing service behind St. James Church in the tent or in an open field. Hundreds of people would attend each day.

Father Rookey is constantly in prayer. Just before leaving Medjugorje to return home, everyone was standing outside waiting for our bus and saying good-by to our host family, When I looked toward Father Rookey he had his hands extended looking at the Miracle of the Sun and praying. I must say I have seen the Miracle of the Sun many, many times before, but never like it was that evening. It was as though Jesus and His Mother Mary were thanking us for coming with the gift of this beautiful display and grand finale.

Margaret M. Trosclair, S.O.S.M.

The Community of the
Secular Order of the Servants of Mary

SECULAR ORDER OF THE SERVANTS OF MARY
St. Anthony Pucci Community, Secular Servites of Louisiana
First in the South

Fr. Peter Mary Rookey, OSM
is pictured in insert

Pictured are all **56 Candidates.**
Seated at center, left to right:
Fr. Donald Mary Siple, OSM
National Director
Fr. Alberto Bermudez
Candidate & Spiritual Director

Immediately behind are members
of **the First Council** left to right:
Darnell Blanchard (in white suit),
Harold Trosclair,
Margaret Trosclair-Prioress,
Gayle Ponseti,
Joyce Trepagnier,
Betty Cushman (in white dress).

Preliminary Meeting - December 17, 1994
Began Formation - January 22, 1995
Rite of Promise - 56 Candidates
January 13, 1996

In 1986, Margaret Trosclair met Fr. Peter Mary Rookey, OSM, for the first time. She was in Medjugorje for the Triumph of the Cross and the Feast of Our Lady of Sorrows. Margaret began working with Fr. Rookey in 1988 when Mary's Helpers hosted his first healing services in the New Orleans area. Because of Fr. Rookey's great devotion to the Mother of Sorrows, we started learning more about her and began sponsoring the Annual Solemn Novena of Our Lady of Sorrows at Immaculate Conception Church in Marrero in 1991.

Fr. Rookey was instrumental in Mary's Helpers beginning the Secular Order of the Servants of Mary in the State of Louisiana. After 7 years of perseverance we were finally accepted. Fr. Rookey was present at the Promise to witness the fruit of his labor. Our community has 15 candidates for the 1997 Promise.

St. Anthony Pucci is the name of our community. Fr. Rookey wrote the book on the life of this Servite saint entitled "The Shepherd of Souls."

We thank Fr. Rookey for his inspiration and for all he has done for us.

Proceeds from this book will be used
to spread the good news that
Jesus Christ
is alive today, just as He was
2,000 years ago.

Printed by *Laborde Printing Company*
516 Frenchman St., New Orleans, Louisiana 70116